Fire ON THE *Earth*

THE ARTS AND THEIR PHILOSOPHIES

a series edited by

JOSEPH MARGOLIS

Fire
ON THE
Earth

ANSELM KIEFER
and the
Postmodern World

John C. Gilmour

Temple University Press

PHILADELPHIA

Temple University Press, Philadelphia 19122
Copyright © 1990 by Temple University. All rights reserved
Published 1990
Printed in the United States of America

The paper used in this publication meets the minimum
requirements of American National Standard for Information
Sciences—Permanence of Paper for Printed Library Materials,
ANSI Z39.48-1984

Library of Congress Cataloging-in-Publication Data
Gilmour, John, 1939–
    Fire on the earth : Anselm Kiefer and the postmodern world / John C.
Gilmour.
        p.   cm. — (The Arts and their philosophies)
    Includes bibliographical references.
    ISBN 0-87722-690-3 (alk. paper)
    1. Kiefer, Anselm, 1945–   —Criticism and interpretation.
    2. Postmodernism.   I. Title.   II. Series.
    ND588.K464G55   1990
    759.3—dc20   89-20137
                                                             CIP

To Sheila, who made it possible

Contents

Illustrations

FIGURES

after page 48

PLATES

after page 176

Preface

FORTUITOUS EVENTS often shape the scholar's agenda, and the present study is no exception. While vacationing in Paris in June, 1984, I strolled into the Musée d'Art Moderne de la Ville de Paris to see if they were showing anything of interest. I was barely prepared for their exhibition of Anselm Kiefer's work, since I knew very little of him at that date. That first encounter made a powerful impression. I found myself haunted by Kiefer's images without really knowing why. Perhaps it was the sheer expressive power they had, deriving in part from their abstract expressionist scale. Yet more was at stake than scale and expressive energy. The dissonant tones created by Kiefer, more troubling than Rothko's darkest canvasses, depended for their force on conflicting signs that resisted easy resolution. They were first indicators of his intellectual astuteness. Figurative, historical, and textual references were interlarded with otherwise abstract painting, mythic themes competed with aesthetic motifs for the viewer's attention, and fragments of prints, bits of debris, and other foreign elements intruded into what should have been pure painting space. And there was more besides. I left intrigued, needing to learn more about Kiefer's work and what motivated him to flaunt formalist strictures.

The encounter with Kiefer was timely, since I had just finished a book, *Picturing the World*, in which I had challenged the formalist understanding of modernism. I recognized in Kiefer a painter whose practices went against the formalist grain. At the same time I noticed his kinship with philosophical themes I had long known in Nietzsche's writings. A few months later I gave a talk contrasting modern humanism with a tragic conception of human nature. My guides had been Nietzsche and J.-P. Vernant, whose analysis of Greek tragedy was a main source for my ideas. When I reflected on Kiefer's work, I was struck by the overlap that existed between his art and the themes I explored in that talk. After seeing more of his work in Toronto at the European Iceberg exhibition in April, 1985, followed the next month by Marian Goodman's showing of Kiefer's "Departure from Egypt" series in New York, I was ready to embark on the present study.

Born in Germany at the close of World War II, Anselm Kiefer represents the concerns and insecurities of postwar European intellectuals, confronted by a questionable past and by a future so threatening that it tends to create despair. One result is loss of confidence in the ideals and way of life inherited from the Enlightenment. Kiefer is no exception to this response. Nevertheless, his tragic outlook reaches beyond a sense of loss and despair. He becomes the advocate of the visionary artist, who will contribute to the renewal and revitalization of history, yet in terms departing from the modern historical ideal. A central goal of the present study is to clarify the way Kiefer's stance departs from modernism and to show how that generates a conflict between his outlook and the received world view of modernity.

Special thanks are due to Joseph Margolis, whose 1980 NEH Summer Seminar on the Concept of Culture in the Philosophy of Art began my intellectual odyssey into the issues defined in this book. His encouragement has contributed greatly to the final outcome. I am grateful, also, for courteous help from Peter d'Jonge, then of the Van Abbemuseum, Eindhoven, Holland and to Marie-Louise Laband of the Anthony d'Offay Gallery in London, both of whom made special arrangements for me to have access to Kiefer's works during a sabbatical leave in 1985–1986.

I am indebted to Margarete Landwehr, whose help with translations has been crucial. She read the roundtable discussion *Ein Gespräch: Joseph Beuys, Janis Kounellis, Anselm Kiefer, and Enzo Cucchi* with me and has done the translations of that work included here. Beyond the translations her knowledge of German culture and of allusions to German literature in the roundtable exchange has contributed materially to my grasp of that discussion.

In addition the book would have been impossible without generous personal and financial support from Alfred University—particularly assistance from Dean John R. Foxen, Dean Chris Gront-kowski, and the NEH Steering Committee, an Alfred University Summer Study grant, and the sabbatical leave. The encouragement given by my colleagues in the Division of Human Studies has also been essential—particularly by Bill Dibrell, who commented on some early material, by Stuart Campbell and Gary Ostrower, for encouragement and for advice about publishing, and by Tom Leddy (a former colleague), who first called my attention to Kiefer, but most of all, by Tom Peterson, with whom I taught a seminar on issues about contemporary culture and whose reading and criticism of the first draft was invaluable.

Substantial editorial help was provided by William G. Wall, whose work on matters of form and style has enhanced the quality of the manuscript, and by Elizabeth Gulacsy, who checked everything for accuracy. Yvonne Cassidy and Sheila Gilmour did the bulk of the proofreading, and Pam Larkin did the majority of the indexing. Without the secretarial help of Barbara Sanford the process of producing this book would have been far more trying. And the assistance of Doris Braendel on copy-editing, Henna Remstein on matters of copyright, and Richard Gilbertie on production has contributed greatly to the final product.

Finally, the project would never have been possible without the unfailing support of my wife, Sheila, who is always the first sounding-board for my ideas and who so often discerns analogies and comparisons that illuminate the material I am developing.

Acknowledgments

THE AUTHOR GRATEFULLY ACKNOWLEDGES permissions from the following: Christopher Middleton, for permission to quote from his translation of Paul Celan's "Fugue of Death"; Berthold Hinz, for supplying the photographic material for Figure 10, which appeared in his book, *Art in the Third Reich* (Oxford, Eng.: Basil Blackwell, 1979); William Eastman, for permission to use material published in my article, "Anselm Kiefer: Postmodern Art and the Question of Technology," in Gary Shapiro (ed.), *After the Future: Postmodern Times and Places* (Albany, N.Y.: SUNY Press, 1990); Roger Shiner, for permission to use material published in my article, "Original Representation and Anselm Kiefer's Postmodernism," *Journal of Aesthetics and Art Criticism* 46, no. 3 (Spring, 1988): 341–355.

In addition, the following credits concerning plates and figures should be noted:

Figure 6   Piet Mondrian, *Trees*, Carnegie Museum of Art, Pittsburgh. Patrons Art Fund.

Figure 15   *Ways of Worldly Wisdom: Arminius's Battle*, The Art Institute, Chicago. Restricted gift of Mr. and Mrs. Noel Rothman, Mr. and Mrs. Douglas Cohen, Mr. and Mrs. Thomas Dittmer, Mr. and Mrs. Lewis Manilow, Mr. and Mrs. Joel Shapiro, Mr. and Mrs. Ralph Goldenberg, and Wirt D. Walker Fund.

Figure 31   *The Order of Angels*, The Art Institute, Chicago. Restricted gift of the Nathan Manilow Foundation and Lewis and Susan Manilow, Samuel A. Marx Fund.

Figure 33   *The Red Sea*, The Museum of Modern Art, New
               York. Enid A. Haupt Fund.

Plate VI   *Midgard*, The Carnegie Museum, Pittsburgh.
               Museum purchase: gift of Kaufmann's, the
               Women's Committee, and the Fellows of the
               Museum of Art, 1985.

Plate X   *Emanation*, Walker Art Center, Minneapolis. Gift of
               Judy and Kenneth Dayton, 1990.

Fire ON THE *Earth*

INTRODUCTION

THE PRESENT STUDY addresses a crisis common to late twentieth-century art and aesthetic theory. This crisis concerns the loss of convictions that once governed the practice of art and the interpretive enterprise associated with it. We no longer feel sure of how to distinguish art from non-art, good from bad art, nor even how to identify what makes a work distinctively modern. Moreover, we have doubts about whether the idea of the modern matters any longer in a culture championing, in the broadest ways, the cult of the new. We discern artists and critics alike practicing their professions in an atmosphere of uncertainty about the direction the history of art is taking, and we seem forced to describe the dominant ethos as pluralistic. Even contemporary philosophy offers little help, since skepticism about the foundations of aesthetic theory seems more symptomatic of the decline of modern culture than a guide to overcoming it. Modernism's historical moment has passed, and the shape of its historical offspring is only now beginning to emerge.

Anselm Kiefer is one of the artists helping to mold a postmodern vision. This case study of Kiefer goes beyond the interpretation of one artist's work, since I believe Kiefer helps reveal the contours of postmodern culture. I have chosen Kiefer because he so well exemplifies currents broadly running in European culture since World War II and because his work confronts the new situation resulting from modernism's decline. Kiefer, who was born in 1945 in Germany, has had to face up to dissolution of the world promised by Enlightenment thought, including the place it assigned to art. Kiefer symbolizes the plight of a whole generation, forced to grapple with the breakdown of received values in response to tragic events in twentieth-century history. He is especially important in

3

this regard because of the forthright way he confronts these tragic circumstances.

There is a fortunate convergence between themes in Kiefer's art and broader discussions within postmodern thought, making his work an ideal vehicle for assessing the relationship between the history of art and the history of philosophy in the present moment. This is especially evident in the way he adapts his art to the play of multiple texts and historical traditions. Like so many of the theorists whose ideas I will associate with Kiefer, his approach is intertextual, drawing freely from a variety of sources to create unsuspected associations and conflicts.

Before proceeding further I want to comment on the free interpretation I give to Kiefer's work. Questions about interpretive procedures are central to postmodern thought, and my own approach to Kiefer deliberately embraces intertextual practices. Whereas the ideal of objectivity often requires a scholar to suppress speculative associations that might otherwise prove fruitful, an intertextual approach cultivates them in the hope of uncovering unsuspected cultural convergences. Such an approach is justified because of the openness of cultural systems. Since practices and ideas are broadly disseminated, a complete comprehension by those who employ them is unlikely at best. Thus, I am less concerned to document an actual influence of the thinkers I discuss on Kiefer than to reveal common cultural currency. This is especially true of my use of Friedrich Nietzsche's ideas to interpret Kiefer. Even though Nietzsche's name is inscribed into at least one of Kiefer's works, the extent of his actual influence on him is less important than the fact that Nietzsche's ideas are broadly disseminated in twentieth-century culture.

My interpretive procedure is not unlike Kiefer's own artistic practice. He draws freely from such diverse sources as the Exodus from Egypt, ideas about the celestial hierarchy in Dionysius the Areopagite, Nordic myths, German military and cultural history, and shamanistic religion. Thus, his postmodern art calls forth my postmodern interpretive practices. A specific case in point will be found in Chapter Three, where I associate Kiefer's theatricality with Antonin Artaud's Theater of Cruelty and with Jacques Der-

rida's idea of "original representation," introduced by Derrida to
clarify Artaud. Rather than claiming that Kiefer actually derived
his practice from Artaud's, I will use the texts of Artaud and Derrida to illuminate Kiefer's texts. This procedure will serve one
main purpose of this study: to establish a close relationship between developments in art and contemporary thought. To this end
I will interweave discussion of Kiefer's works with such thinkers
as Derrida, Michel Foucault, Gilles Deleuze and Felix Guattari,
Jean Baudrillard, Jean-François Lyotard, Peter Bürger, and Fredric
Jameson. Just as they have challenged leading tenets of the inherited
intellectual tradition, so Kiefer's work confronts the leading assumptions of modernist practice and criticism.

Kiefer moves beyond modernism by violating its taboos against
representation, narrative, and historical allusion and by the decisive
way in which he employs art to confront reality. At the same time,
he raises fundamental doubts about the received world view of
modernity (a term I will employ for the complex of ideas inherited
from the Enlightenment). Although the avant-garde were radical
in their criticism of bourgeois society and of the institutions of
the art world, Kiefer's challenge extends further toward the roots
of modern humanity's outlook. He does so by turning the canvas
into a theater of interacting forces that expose tragic conflicts engendered by modern life. By synthesizing the traditional and the
modern, the mythological and the rational, the simulated and the
real, Kiefer achieves a puzzling and provocative mixture of elements that inspire us to reconsider our assumptions and formulate
our visions anew.

To begin, let us consider Kiefer's 1975 painting entitled *Operation "Seelöwe"* (Plate I). While this painting appears to revive the
landscape tradition, it opens up a strange scene for us to contemplate. The land itself seems constituted by the soldiers' bodies,
whose individual forms are visible or implied, yet overpainted so
as to convey the abstract impression of a single collective mass.
At the center of the canvas a large, elongated tub rests, filled with
water on which three ships are afloat, with a flame ignited above
the one in the middle. Overarching the scene, three empty orange
chairs, whose color reiterates that of the flame below, rest on a

transparent platform, giving the appearance that they rule over the soldiers, the ships, and the landscape. What strange scene is this, which makes use of the conventions of realistic representation without giving us a familiar reality to contemplate?

We must notice, immediately, Kiefer's penchant for undermining comfortable readings, taking away with one hand what he gives with the other. We have no doubt that Kiefer is a *modern* painter, even though he represents tub, ship, soldiers, and chair in recognizable ways, since the moving flow of colors around the tub works like an abstract expressionist field, the overpainting obscuring otherwise realistic elements and transforming them into something else. What seemed at first glance like a window opening onto reality is unlike any we have looked through in search of the everyday. There can be no doubt that these artist's gestures are calculated to provoke thought and to stimulate questions about our basic assumptions.

In this respect Kiefer is a *philosophical* painter. He creates a Socratic engagement with the familiar, undermining our confidence that we know what we are seeing. A painting neither abstract nor realistic, a painting whose references to physical reality and history get undermined by imaginary features, a painting where language intrudes onto the painted surface ("Unternehmen Seelöwe") as an element in the formal composition: these are only a few of the respects in which Kiefer's painting practice calls for further analysis.

The return to representation in postmodern painting is, in fact, the first element subject to misinterpretation. If we think of representation in the received way, then the contrast between objective depiction and abstraction creates an unbridgeable gulf. Kiefer *shows* that this dichotomy, around which so much modernist interpretation has been built, is untenable. In the case of *Operation "Seelöwe,"* the surface is transparent and opaque simultaneously, casting doubt upon the modernist conviction of an opposition between the two pictorial modes. What Kiefer has accomplished here is the creation of a *fictional* perspective by using some of the practices of realistic representation to create an imaginary space. Donald Kuspit sees this as a feature of postmodern German painting in general:

It is not merely a matter of reaffirming referentiality and the hierarchy of figure-ground relationships. Rather, it is a matter of creating a fictional reference, of which the figure is the instrument, to create an illusion of being-natural. The creation of this illusion—to bring into question the artificiality of art and technological society—is a major critical aspect of the new German painting.[1]

This critical thrust raises questions about the modernist conception of the artist's role within contemporary society, about how we conceive the relation between pictures and reality, and extends, in Kiefer's case especially, to historical reflections on the forms of power shaping our age. Thus, his creation of fictional scenes dramatizes issues both about our world view and about our politics.

What makes me speak of Kiefer as an example of the philosophical painter? I have in mind the Socratic philosopher, who probes from within an existing tradition to expose its assumptions and limitations, creating a path or direction for ongoing development of that tradition. It is clear that Kiefer's art tradition is modernism, the core of which includes emphasis upon the immediate presence of the pictorial surface and upon techniques for expanding its expressive power. Rightly or wrongly, many of the practitioners of modernism believed that they had to resist all representational and historical references in order to promote that immediacy. Kiefer's own ironic response is to create works having obvious expressive power but exposing, as well, the hidden textuality and historical grounding entering into every form of painting practice. He does so in a variety of ways. In *Operation "Seelöwe,"* he mixes the use of referential and abstract elements, detaching some of the objects referred to from any easy, consistent reading.

Before proceeding further we must clarify Kiefer's relationship to modernist painting practices. If we understand modernism the way Clement Greenberg does, this cultural movement fits naturally within the world view of modernity. He views modernist painting within the specialist outlook of modernity, where each discipline has its own unique domain. In the case of painting its domain is the two-dimensional surface, and, thus, the exploration of the various aspects of flatness is the proper concern of the modernist painter. For Greenberg it follows that the modernist painter must avoid all *associations* with objects in three-dimensional space, even though he denies that representation per se is prohibited. The danger is that such associations will, as he says, "alienate pictorial space from the two-dimensionality which is the guarantee of painting's independence as an art. Three-dimensionality is the province of sculpture, and for the sake of its own autonomy painting has had above all to divest itself of everything it might share with sculpture."[2] Kiefer's work is a self-conscious rejection of a view of painting like Greenberg's since, like so many postmodern artists, he employs a multi-media approach, mixing sculptural, photographic, and print elements into his paintings. In addition, he violates another feature of Greenberg's claim that "modernist painting asks that a literary theme be translated into strictly optical, two-dimensional terms before becoming the subject of pictorial art—which means its being translated in such a way that it entirely loses its literary character,"[3] since he deliberately evokes literary and historical images for purposes beyond painting itself. The autonomy of art forms is anything but a compelling issue for him.

Some aspects of Kiefer's procedure are very complex. He merges his reconsideration of modernist painting practices with his critical examination of his own German heritage. For example, *Operation "Seelöwe"* has its historical grounding in a planning operation by Hitler's generals during World War II, the title being the code name for an attack on England that never materialized.[4] Kiefer experimented in his studio with the planning scenario, simulating the map exercise by setting up a lead tub filled with water at varying levels on which he floated toy ships and chunks of ice. He created several paintings based on these simulations, as well as a number of books of photographs depicting various aspects of this studio experiment. Kiefer's *modus operandi* displays something of the complex view he has of the artist's imagination, which in many ways resembles the imaginary powers of the generals, who, though absent from their chairs on the elevated platform, still exercise power over the collective mass below.

More broadly, Kiefer raises questions about the power that

ideas and imagined scenarios have over the collective life of a people, forming myths that provide an identity and a basis for action. Even when these mythical powers operate in silence, their power is nevertheless very real. Kiefer believes that if art is to fulfill its potential for bringing about change, a realistic confrontation of these powers is necessary. They cannot be overcome by simple acts of negation, since many negative gestures end up, in fact, perpetuating those things they are intended to remove. For example, attempts by modern artists to purify art by rejecting the values of a materialistic culture may have served only to isolate artists from any effective role with the general public. As well intentioned as anti-representational and anti-materialistic gestures may have been, their outcome may, nevertheless, be unacceptable. One reason Kiefer mixes representational and abstract elements is because they allow him to use historical associations without any loss of the artist's ability to maintain a critical stance toward that history. This mixture enables him to formulate ironies and pose problems about the operations of sign systems within art that would otherwise be impossible.

The postmodern use of representation is calculated to raise questions about pictorial images and about representation itself. And in Kiefer's case we find him creating an interplay between representational and modernist conventions that pose questions about both. In addition, it enables the postmodern artist to probe the borderline that supposedly divides reality from simulation by using reality-elements to pose questions about reality. While many artists achieve this effect through fragmentation devices, Kiefer achieves his within *Operation "Seelöwe"* by synthesizing conflicting interpretations within what appears to be a single scene: not literally, like an Escher print does, but metaphorically. Thus, the soldiers *compose* the land on which they stand, the transparent platform controlling their movements as if a god ruled over them, the toy tub and ships, commanding center stage, making clear that map-exercise games may create momentous consequences. The whole effect is of a simulated scene whose actuality is in doubt, the location of the tub being made to appear, in some respects, as resting on the ground, while in others as floating above the head and shoulders of the troops. The net effect is to raise doubts about what is reality and what is interpretation.

The vantage point of my philosophical investigation into postmodern culture reflects my conviction that works of art should be at the center of aesthetic analysis, serving to generate categories of interpretation, rather than serving as illustrations for the epistemological convictions already embraced by the philosopher. For this purpose, I will focus on the works of Anselm Kiefer as the primary source for my reflections on postmodern culture, not because he provides the basis for a generally valid *definition* of the postmodern, but because his work is a rich source for questions we must confront in coming to understand developments in the visual arts since the 1960s. Not only does he challenge some of the leading critical ideas about modernism, but he also actively employs ancient historical sources, the practices of the alchemist, mythological and cosmological narratives, and his own German tradition to undermine modern assumptions of universal knowledge, historical progress, and a purely aesthetic role for the arts. While I believe that these features of Kiefer's work link themselves to other postmodern developments, which collectively challenge our understanding of modernity, it is too early to claim that they herald a new *age* in Western culture. Indeed, such a claim will be seen to be misplaced, given the analysis of history that will unfold in the following chapters.

Moreover, claims about eras in cultural development are subject to serious distortion, as astute analysts like Peter Bürger have shown with respect to the intrusion of broad ideological categories into cultural analysis. Thus, while it may be true that contemporary art reflects the history of bourgeois society in general ways, it is a mistake to take particular developments, such as Kiefer's return to the historical past and to Germanic myths, as a sign of a reactionary response to bourgeois conditions. Such an approach is mistaken because, as Bürger has argued, our categories of interpretation develop alongside the historical changes they eventually make comprehensible.[5] This is as true within the arts as outside them. If, for example, the development of the proletariat as a class was necessary before the *category* of the proletariat could emerge as a plausible interpretive concept, so may some practices of post-modern artists be antecedent to the categories they give rise to and the criticisms they make possible. Bürger's own example concerns the way the category of the avant-garde has functioned within cultural interpretation. While some interpreters, operating from a broadly ideological perspective, treated the avant-garde as ful-filling revolutionary purposes against bourgeois society, Bürger sees its achievement as the unmasking of earlier forms of devel-opment within art, providing *us* with a new basis for criticism. The avant-garde shows us, therefore, an outcome of art institu-tions that gathered themselves around the ideal of purely aesthetic art. It does so in two ways: the Dadaist focus on artistic means *as* means brings to the surface a feature inherent in the idea of purely aesthetic art (one divorced from serving religious meaning or the functions of the king's court, for example); and gestures such as the Marcel Duchamp urinal, designed as they were to destroy art as an institution, have been absorbed into the very institutions they were directed against (Duchamp in the museum). While the avant-garde emphasis upon artistic means *as* means has now lost its force as an instrument of criticism, since creations featuring this aspect of art have become highly successful and profitable within the current art scene, the historical avant-garde may, nevertheless, provide a model for ironic commentary within contemporary art.

Bürger himself is skeptical about attempts of the neo-avant-garde (Andy Warhol, for example) to revitalize the avant-garde program of an attack upon art as an institution. Rather, Bürger believes that the correct lesson of history is that the era of the avant-garde is over.[6] The real basis for criticism, he thinks, rests with what we can derive from the avant-garde as a category of in-terpretation: our understanding must now include a grasp of just how deeply modern art, including its avant-garde practices, has been implicated in the perpetuation of bourgeois values. A key in-strument in this appropriation of art by modern society is the very idea modernists cherish the most: the autonomy of art, devoted solely to aesthetic purposes.

What this line of reasoning suggests, therefore, is that contem-porary art, if it would serve as a fundamental critique of bourgeois institutions, must go beyond a purely aesthetic art and its counter-part, the ironic exposure of its institutionalization. This new criti-cism must extend toward the undermining of the whole world view within which modern art is assigned its restricted institu-tional place. In Kiefer's case, we find critics divided between those who denounce his work as a betrayal of the avant-garde program and those who see his return to the past and to mythic sources as the necessary instrument for a fundamental critique of the mod-ern world view. In contrast, neo-avant-garde gestures may, despite their intentions, serve only to perpetuate that world view. Never-theless, Bürger's warning about cultural evaluation reiterates itself here, since we have no definitive way to evaluate whether the post-modern return to references, historical allusions, and mythological perspectives will, in fact, undermine or reinforce established his-torical institutions, especially since they resemble in some respects forms of nostalgia within contemporary culture. My vantage point is that Kiefer's work escapes the nostalgia trap, provoking us to rethink the significance of the past and of the various mythologies that shape our outlook.

In addition to this issue, the question of whether postmod-ern art is simply a later phase within modernism needs to be addressed. We will discover that significant strands within mod-ernism prefigure developments within Kiefer's work. Treating his works as simply the newest and latest development within mod-ernism, however, would rob them of a part of their power. One major thrust of Kiefer's art is to illuminate and enrich our under-standing of history by using it in unexpected ways. The very idea of history as it occurs within the world view of modernity is very much at issue, as we shall see in later chapters.

This topic is an important one for cultural interpretation in gen-eral. As Peter Bürger sees it, we have a strong tendency to interpret developments within art in terms of a pre-existing idea of the his-tory of bourgeois society, rather than letting them help shape our conception of history. He adds that "where that history is taken as an already known reference system and used as such in the histori-cal investigation of partial social spheres, cultural science degen-erates into a procedure of establishing correspondences."[7] That is what we do when we simply see the postmodern as the newest and latest form of the modern. In effect, we reduce the postmodern to the modern and disarm it from its ability to sketch out a different historical understanding. Such a move is profoundly misleading in Kiefer's case, as we will see particularly since a major thrust of his work mounts a challenge to our inherited idea of historical progress.

While some may see the focus on Kiefer's work as too restrictive for a general understanding of postmodern developments, I believe that he raises sufficiently provocative questions about the received tradition of modernism to shed significant light, retrospectively, on the practices of modernism. His work cuts to the heart of the connection that binds modernism to the world view of modernity. This connection is evident in a critic like Greenberg, who highlights the way modernist art has a "convergence of spirit with science" because of the common commitment they have to specialization.[8] Greenberg says:

> Scientific method alone asks that a situation be resolved in exactly the same kind of terms as that in which it is presented—a problem in physiology is solved in terms of physiology, not in those of psychology; to be solved in terms of psychology, it has to be presented in, or translated into, these terms first.[9]

By fostering the idea of purely aesthetic art, modernists have perpetuated this outlook, which Greenberg seems to regard as a virtue. One reason for focusing on Kiefer's work is the degree to which he challenges this assumed virtue and poses an alternative by his use of pre-scientific forms of thought (such as alchemy). At the same time, his work has sufficient concordance with other postmodern artists to serve as one avenue toward a more general understanding of postmodern culture. And finally, Kiefer's painting has one additional advantage for my own understanding of postmodern culture, since many of his own concerns overlap with theoretical concerns of Nietzsche and the poststructuralists. Their approaches to culture represent the best chance we have of understanding developments within the postmodern moment. Yet some of them take insufficient cognizance of cosmological questions that are crucial for contemporary humans. In this respect, Kiefer helps to expose a limitation in the approach of certain postmodern theorists.

Part I will consider what Kiefer's return to representational practices means. His use of representational images contrasts with their role from the Renaissance until the late nineteenth century. This change arises from an altered conception of reality: representational images once mirrored nature but now often manifest the effect of simulated environments and humanly designed spaces. I will consider Kiefer's work against the background of ideas from Nietzsche, Michel Foucault, and Jean Baudrillard, since they all sketch out alternatives to modernity's limited idea of the real. Part I concludes with a comparison between Kiefer's practices and Jacques Derrida's notion of "original representation," a concept he introduces to help us understand Artaud's ideas about the Theater of Cruelty. This theme links Kiefer's tendency toward the tragic with pre-modern forms of thought having the potential to enrich our conception of reality.

Since the idea of the creative subject in modernism arises from our understanding of the difference between objective reality and the human subject, Kiefer's creation of a form of "original representation" points toward an altered conception of human experience and action. Part II considers the shift from modernity's conception of the individual subject to the contemporary emphasis on the text. Whereas modernism conceives the artist as expressing an individual perspective through the work, postmodern thought conceives the artist as achieving personal identity through the play of textual interpretations. I consider how such an approach alters our understanding of the past and how Kiefer's art employs cosmological, mythical, and historical narratives to challenge our preconceptions about humanity and the world. A major subtheme within this discussion is the way Kiefer's tragic vision helps to unmask repressed features of the past that our idea of historical progress obscures. Although Kiefer's own emphasis is often on the German past, the effect of his unmasking gestures is to challenge the Enlightenment dream of a rational history through showing us the power myths and other forms of narrative exert over our thinking. In this section the thought of Nietzsche, Fredric Jameson, and Jean-François Lyotard play a large role.

Finally, Part III considers the larger implications of Kiefer's art for our understanding of the postmodern moment. His tragic outlook and his probing of cosmological themes raise questions about the modern understanding of history and the human habitat. Both of these challenges gain direction from Kiefer's examination of technology in relation to alchemy and other ancient practices. The book closes with a reconsideration of the importance of simulation systems in the contemporary world and the illumination we gain on these issues from Kiefer's work.

The guiding theme of the investigation is that Kiefer's postmodern art clarifies issues left unresolved within modernism and sheds light on leading conceptual questions that relate to the postmodern world. Kiefer, schooled in the atmosphere of postwar Germany, may have had to confront questions about the modern world view sooner than most, but his locally based perspective is no more limited than our own, representing as it does a fragmentary perspective whose validity depends upon the power it has to reveal reality.

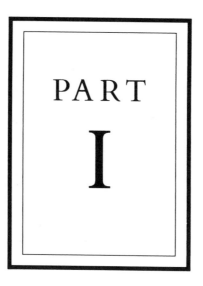

PART

I

Representation and

Simulation in

Postmodern Art

CHAPTER ONE

Windows, Mirrors, and Grids

WE HAVE SEEN that Kiefer creates visual dissonance in *Operation "Seelöwe"* by mixing the modes of representation, thereby interfering with our desire to unify the scene into a coherent totality. His undermining of an organic whole-part relationship within visual reality is central to his strategy as a postmodern painter, since he repeatedly creates conflicts for the viewer by playing to our visual predispositions, while simultaneously suspending them in other respects. The resulting tension exposes the role these predisposing attitudes play in our visual experience. Other examples will clarify just how sophisticated Kiefer's approach is to the visible world, making it possible for him to generate questions and uncertainties that extend very far.

Kiefer's painting *To the Supreme Being* (Figure 1) offers a rich basis on which to begin our analysis. Kiefer confronts us with an empty brick shell that looks as if it had once been a room, or as if it were about to become one, housing some significant function. It looks more like a warehouse than like a cathedral, more like an abandoned prison than a hall for festive celebration. We are completely enclosed within its visual space, the only contact with the outside being the faint light penetrating the opaque white panels on the left. There is no furniture, no decoration, no altar or stage —just an empty space. Nevertheless, this haunted hall reminds us of something familiar, something that echoes faintly within the recesses of memory. What makes this image so arresting, even as Mark Rothko's empty abstractions often are?

The sedimented layers of significance buried within this seemingly simple image will require attentive analysis before this question can be answered adequately. For one thing, the latticed ceiling reverberates with visual conventions etched deeply within our collective memory, as will become evident by reference to Leonardo da Vinci's *The Last Supper* (Figure 2). Not only does Kiefer's ceiling reiterate the structure of Leonardo's ceiling, but the three black panels at the end of Kiefer's chamber strike one as analogues to the background windows in Leonardo's upper room, except that Kiefer's background spaces are covered over in black. In addition, Kiefer's walls, though made of brick rather than of plaster, contain panels shaping the recession toward the back, similar in appearance to those on Leonardo's walls. It is as if Kiefer has simply removed us further from the back, elongating the space to dramatize the emptiness. Kiefer's painting gives us no scene: no table, no Christ and his disciples, no food, and no windows opening onto nature. Only the room itself, where nothing is happening, opens out before us, and we cannot even tell what function this space has been designed to hold. What appears at first as a return to the practices of Alberti's Window,* opening up the visual space along the lines of perspective recession, eventually contradicts the expectations those practices normally support. The floor in this fantasy space is not even solid, since it appears more like the mirrored reflection of the ceiling above (but without so much light) than like a real floor. Like the mirror rooms created by recent artists, where floor, ceiling, and walls reflect the same image from various directions, Kiefer's room presents a reflexive chamber within which visualizing and revisualizing occur in terms of their own laws.

We must gather several strands together before we can discover the full range of Kiefer's visual intelligence reflected in this haunting image. We must consider, first of all, the way he interweaves the return to representation with the self-conscious gestures of modernist practices. This synthesis requires, especially, that we reconsider the opposition modernists have assumed between representation and abstraction, particularly when they have highlighted

---

*This term refers to the ideas of Leon Baptista Alberti, whose *Della Pittura* (published in 1436) gives the first clear statement of the principles of the Renaissance perspective system. The "window" in question refers to the illusion that we are seeing real things through the picture surface.

the way abstraction can liberate painting from the limitations inherent in picturing things. To approach this reconsideration, we must examine received dogmas about representation and consider the challenge posed to them within postmodern art. Similarly, other strands of our analysis will challenge other modernist assumptions. For example, we will ask what relationship the inscription "to the supreme being," appearing in the lower right, bears to the rest of the painting. Why is this text inscribed within the painted space, which is supposed, according to modernist dictum, to be preserved for vision alone? This text is just one example among many of Kiefer's use of language within his paintings. We shall ask, as well, why the blank spaces appear at the end of the chamber, just where a scene or important symbol might be. What sort of space is this that Kiefer has created, a space whose power derives as much from what has been removed as from what appears within its confines? All of these questions will enter into the present chapter.

If we consider the question of representation first, we are on the brink of a serious misunderstanding if we treat either Kiefer's haunted hall or Leonardo's upper room as instances of the picture surface serving primarily as a perspective window. The idea that the primary role of visual representation is to depict objects of the real world by the illusion of a painted window omits many other factors that must come into serious thought about visual representation. In the case of Leonardo, while it is true that he displays a mastery of Filippo Brunelleschi's perspective laws in his depiction of the upper room, the realism this enables him to achieve is not the only, or even the primary, issue attached to the power of his work. In fact, our historical grasp of Leonardo's representation gets distorted immediately if we think of Alberti's Window as opening onto an objective world, understood in the terms of the scientific world view. Although Leonardo contributed materially to the emergence of that world view through his own detailed nature studies and experiments, *The Last Supper* is more dramatic and religious than it is objective. The expressive elements contained in Leonardo's depiction of the scene, although perhaps heightened by the convincing realism of the space, are more central

to the work than any objective vantage point alleged to characterize Renaissance representational practices. Foucault has shown that
the archaeological structures undergirding sixteenth-century culture reflect a distinctly different set of assumptions from those that
flower in the seventeenth and eighteenth centuries (what Foucault
calls the Classical age). Thus, Foucault sees questions of resemblance, analogy, adjacency, emulation, and sympathy entering into
the practices of sixteenth-century thinkers and artists in ways to be
denied by the objective stance of seventeenth-century philosophy,
science, and art.[1] In part, this approach of Leonardo's era reflects
the continuing influence of the ancient world view, according to
which any portion of reality is a microcosm of the macrocosm,
even when it appears to be far removed from the whole. The play
of analogy, adjacency, emulation, and sympathy are all clear in the
case of *The Last Supper* if we remember its location on the refectory wall in the monastery for which it was painted (Figure 3).
Our well-established tendency to isolate the painting *as* a painting obscures the role of this play of resemblances for Leonardo's
contemporaries. This is one of the consequences of our own preoccupation with a purely aesthetic art.

A little analysis will clarify the features of resemblance-thinking
that enter into Leonardo's work. When we remember the role
of the painting within the architectural space it occupied, we remember that it rose above the space where monks dined. Thus,
Leonardo's painting of Jesus dining with his disciples sets up resonances and resemblances within the setting where Christian monks
dine together. Their refectory space becomes a microcosm of the
holy space of the upper room, which is also itself supposed to
be a microcosm of the conflicts between a humanly understood
world and the one ruled over by God. The painting, appearing as
it might over the head table of the monastery, where the abbot
rules as the representative of Jesus, is representational primarily
through its being *representative* within its world view. The painted
upper room, rising above the monks within the architectural space,
has striking affinities, as well, with the transparent platform rising
above the soldiers in Kiefer's *Operation "Seelöwe."* While the imaginations of the monks may have been enhanced by the realism of

the setting, including the resemblance of the painted space to their own architectural space, what is of unsurpassed importance in the painting is its religious and dramatic content, not its reflection of Brunelleschi's laws.

What this example shows us is that Kiefer's use of earlier practices of visual representation raises issues beyond objective versus non-objective depiction. His return to representation does not, in and of itself, say anything about the reaffirmation of rationalist or scientific values. While Kiefer may not have actually intended to set off these reverberations between *To the Supreme Being* and Leonardo's *The Last Supper*, the comparison remains visually important and instructive. The juxtaposition of the title with the empty space also says much about the removal of religious mythology from a central place within our own culture. *What* it says may be open to debate, but it would surely be foolish to assume that Kiefer's sophisticated gesture exhibits a nostalgic wish to return to a monkish condition. On the contrary, its power is more diagnostic than nostalgic, the black panels at the end of the chamber seeming to erase the altar or stained glass window that might hold that space if we were in a cathedral.

The diagnostic thrust of Kiefer's act of negation will become clear if we make another sort of comparison, one that seems more pertinent to the actual power to haunt us that the painting has. What I have in mind is Nietzsche's passage in *The Gay Science* depicting a madman who rushed into the market place with a lantern:

> The madman jumped into their midst and pierced them with his eyes. "Whither is God?" he cried; "I will tell you. *We have killed him*—you and I. All of us are his murderers. But how did we do this? How could we drink up the sea? Who gave us the sponge to wipe away the entire horizon? What were we doing when we unchained this earth from its sun? Whither is it moving now? Whither are we moving? Away from all suns? Are we not plunging continually? Backward, sideward, forward, in all directions? Is there still any up or down? Are we not straying as through an infinite nothing? Do we not feel the breath of empty space? . . . Do we smell nothing as yet of the divine decomposition? Gods, too, decompose. God is dead. God remains dead. And we have killed him."[2]

The negativity of Kiefer's painted chamber suggests this "breath of empty space." The ironic inscription, "to the supreme being," suggests the death of God as well. As Nietzsche's rhetorical questions and metaphors make clear, the madman's diagnostic judgment is tied to his perception of what has occurred as the result of the change of world view from Leonardo's day to our own. Nietzsche concludes the story of the madman with another observation:

> It has been related further that on the same day the madman forced his way into several churches and there struck up his *requiem aeternam deo*. Led out and called to account, he is said always to have replied nothing but: "What after all are these churches now if they are not the tombs and sepulchers of God?"[3]

Kiefer appears to have presented a visualization of such a tomb, emptied out like the bombed ruins of World War II buildings, leaving only the specter of an empty space, charged with resonances from the past. Kiefer makes clear, as well, just how far removed we are from the world view of Leonardo and the monks, our contemporary monasteries appearing to us as anachronistic institutions in a world hostile to all they represent.

Foucault has shown that the gap between Leonardo and the thinkers of the Classical age (seventeenth and eighteenth centuries) is also great. Foucault argues that the thinkers of this later age aspired to an ideal of representation as *transparency*, according to which anything represented has such a clear role in the objective world that its meaning is without ambiguity or uncertainty. Foucault notes that such an ideal of clarity can only be achieved through an interlocking network of ideas that contrasts sharply with sixteenth-century forms.[4] What gives the transparency ideal its force is the notion that everything fits within a law-governed whole, accessible for rational discernment. In contrast, the meaning of *The Last Supper* for the monks is anything but transparent, whatever its spatial conventions may suggest. In part, this is because the rich system of resemblances, analogies, emulations, and so on entails an overdetermination of meaning that makes transparency impossible. Therefore, even though the spatial structure makes evident the geometric grids for anyone who has eyes to see, the significance of the geometry in the representation of the scene, and in its setting within the refectory, is decidedly different than it was for the measurement-and-order theorists of the Classical age.[5] Whereas geometric and mathematical organization is essential to the pursuit of *order* in the Classical age, the role of geometry within ancient and medieval thought is decidedly different, providing the basis for them to detect resemblances and analogies across distances not bridged by natural laws. Thus, a scientist of the sixteenth century, such as Johannes Kepler, could become obsessed with the geometric order of the heavens in ways that sharply contrast with the later uses of mathematical thought, since Kepler's own sense of mathematical order reflects Pythagorean numerological elements that are as much mystical as they are scientific.[6] The critical consideration, therefore, is the use to which the geometric order is put. What is seen through Alberti's Window may be at variance with what will later be seen in the mirror of nature aspired to by the artists and scientists of the Classical age.

If what is seen through Alberti's Window is a microcosm of the macrocosm, and if that macrocosm is conceived as sacred space, or as a space governed by God, then the mode of knowledge it conveys is closer, as Foucault argues, to divination than to rational representation as conceived in the Classical age.[7] That is why Foucault treats Velasquez's *Las Meninas* as the typical manifestation of Classical age representation practices. Velasquez portrays himself and his canvas as within the space of representation, making the canvas much more into a mirror than into a simple window. The mirror image here suggests the internalization of particular representations within the matrix of the representational system. Velasquez self-consciously displays the complexity of this shift through his humorous inclusion of himself looking out at both the subjects being painted (the King and Queen) and at the viewers of the painting. Moreover, Velasquez doubles the irony of the mirror function by including the images of the King and Queen in a mirror on the back wall, completing the visual circuit set up by mirroring and painting. The complex relationships this painting acknowledges within representation in the Classical age are far removed from the directness of analogy in Leonardo's work. Any

transparency the thinkers of the Classical age may have attributed
to visual representation depends, we can see, upon the mediation
processes of a visual system often concealed from our view.

When we examine Kiefer's synthesis of traditional modes of
representation with twentieth-century abstraction practices, we
need to remind ourselves of the alternatives present within various
kinds of representation systems. The difference between the directness of Alberti's Window and the transparency achieved via a universal system of order in the Classical age is not the only difference
we need to note. For while the presence of the grid within painting
is evident in both Leonardo and Kiefer, the grid that Kiefer employs resonates with the practices of modernist abstraction. This
factor is obvious if we shift to another of Kiefer's paintings titled
Piet Mondrian—Arminius's Battle (Figure 4). We encounter the upright form of a tree trunk, overpainted in various ways, the most
striking of which is the superimposed black grid that appears in the
upper section of the painting. Kiefer's reference to Mondrian in
the title indicates directly part of what he intends, since Mondrian
originally arrived at his geometric abstractions after eliminating
content references from his paintings of trees. Compare, for example, three of Mondrian's paintings (Figures 5, 6, and 7) that
exhibit the successive stages of abstraction that develop into the
grid paintings. Kiefer, in putting back the tree that Mondrian had
gradually removed, creates an overdetermined image, reversing
the movement toward austerity and silence characteristic of one
aspect of modern art (that aspect eventuating in Ad Reinhardt's
black canvases and the works of his minimalist compatriots).

The question of how to interpret these grids now requires that
we remember what has already been shown about differences in
representation between the Renaissance and the Classical age. In
an earlier book, *Picturing the World*, I have argued that, although we
can distinguish natural from cultural aspects of seeing, all human
vision is irreducibly cultural.[8] Rather than repeat that analysis here,
I shall simply note the difference between a psychologically based
account of perception, defended by a theorist like Rudolf Arnheim, and the cultural-historical approach favored by interpreters
like Foucault. Arnheim treats the grid as psychologically funda-

mental, as constituting an instinctive conceptual basis entering into all our perceptions. His sophisticated analysis in *The Power of the Center* is impressive in its demonstration of the many structures entering into Western visual practices, structures so fundamental that we often completely overlook them. For the most part, Arnheim treats these structures as reflecting one of two systems: the Cartesian grid, which provides the basis for objective placement within a homogeneous network of right-angled lines, forming the extensive continuum; and a system of radial order, which enables us to establish hierarchies within the continuum by making use of concentric circles to give the highest visual value to what is at the center.[9] Arnheim believes that he has articulated the structures by which visual intuitions get spontaneously organized, indicating the law-like behavior of visual forces.[10] This has the convenient result that visual intuitions correspond with geometrical and mechanical determinations, making for a close fit between perception and scientific theory. Arnheim takes his model from science: "Geometry uses ruler and compass as tools of intellectual construction. Mechanically one can determine the center of an object by weight."[11] This interface between geometry and mechanics gives the basis for derivative visual conventions, according to which *visual* weighting can be achieved through centering and through visual vectors that create an implied gravity or an implied direction of movement. Thus it is that our traditional conception of representation is of something neutral and culture-free.

With Foucault's help, however, we have been able to see why Arnheim's account needs to be relativized to a particular era of cultural history that in many respects has continued from the Classical age until now. It is a cultural structure that values order and calculability above everything else. Martin Heidegger notes to what extent the whole research project of modern Western humans depends upon just these factors:

> Knowing, as research, calls whatever is to account with regard to the way in which and the extent to which it lets itself be put at the disposal of representation. Research has disposal over anything that is when it can either calculate it in its future course in advance or verify a calculation about its past. Nature, in being calculated in advance,

and history, in being historiographically verified as past, become, as it were, "set in place [gestellt]." Nature and history become the objects of a representing that explains. . . . Only that which becomes object in this way is—is considered to be in being.[12]

Two points are critical for our purposes from this passage in Heidegger: the purpose of the mode of representation (explanation) helps to determine what counts as representative, and the mode of representation itself enters into the determination of what is real.

What significance does all of this have for our consideration of Kiefer's Mondrian-tree? Just this: once it is clear that a system of representation may vary with different purposes, the presence of the grid guarantees nothing in particular, except that one knows how to superimpose order wherever it is needed. While the move toward abstraction within modern art may be portrayed as a higher stage of conceptual development, in which the logical processes themselves become subject to pictorial treatment,[13] Kiefer's reintroduction of the tree, dropped out by Mondrian, denies this alleged progressive gain. Why? The issues buried beneath the surface here require a bit of untangling.

We must remember that the Cartesian grid, featured by Arnheim in his analysis of art, was essentially an analytical device, resulting from the desire in the Classical age to explain phenomena in terms of simple foundation elements. At the heart of the genius of this age, as Foucault sees it, is the shift from natural signs, which remain somewhat obscure because they are fragmentary and intermittent, to conventional or arbitrary signs, which yield more readily to systematization. One way in which this shift manifests itself is the whole status accorded to language. As Foucault sees it: "The Renaissance came to a halt before the brute fact that language existed: in the density of the world, a graphism mingling with things or flowing beneath them; marks made upon manuscripts or the pages of books."[14] That view made commentary and exegesis a central part of their intellectual life. Foucault sees the seventeenth century as creating a different view, making language into a function within representation, since thought has the power "to represent itself, that is, to analyse itself by juxtaposing itself to itself, part by part, under the eye of reflection."[15] This means that, by clever design, a sign system can become the basis for transparent or self-evident representation. Foucault adds: "An arbitrary system of signs must permit the analysis of things into their simplest elements; it must be capable of decomposing them into their very origins; but it must also demonstrate how combinations of those elements are possible, and permit the ideal genesis of the complexity of things."[16] For the Classical age, of course, the opposition between arbitrary and natural signs is softened, since they consistently portrayed their projected analytical system as mirroring nature, the sign of which is the mathematical definition of natural laws. This is because they believed that, "in its perfect state, the system of signs is that simple, absolutely transparent language which is capable of naming what is elementary; it is also that complex of operations which defines all possible conjunctions."[17] This means that the right analytic instruments make possible the ideal synthesis of knowledge.

We can see the importance of Foucault's analysis for our grasp of modern art once we note that an artist like Mondrian adapts the ideal of a simple sign system to his own purposes. He employs it to create an opaque surface (the opposite of the Classical age ideal), requiring that we respond imaginatively to the presented image. Contrary to the transparency ideal, modern artists have employed sign systems to raise doubts about the priority the Classical age gave to an idea of fixed reality. Mondrian's use of the grid is one indication of this shift in outlook.

Rosalind Krauss has argued that the grid has become the central conceptual underpinning for modernism.[18] Its prominence in Mondrian, coupled with his emphasis upon primary colors, lends support to the idea that it is the elements of visual analysis that are coming to the fore in modern art. Although later modernists became focused on the visual and logical processes themselves, treating the grid as a central element of autonomous art, earlier modernists like Mondrian and Vassily Kandinsky conceived it as giving rise to a universal art that has spiritual value. In attempting to break art away from the materialistic preoccupations of bourgeois society, these early modernists were far removed from the scientific culture that first made geometric thinking central.[19]

If we follow Krauss in treating the grid as emblematic of the program of modernism, we must exercise caution in generalizing this idea uncritically. Whereas the grid *appears* in all three phases of the art we have considered, although more silently in the art of the Classical age than in the art of Leonardo or Albrecht Dürer, its use in these different periods may point toward different theoretical possibilities, even as it may within modern art itself. Perhaps more typical than the spiritualism of a Mondrian or a Kandinsky has been the desire of modernists to defend the autonomy of art and its isolation from other forms of meaning. Krauss speaks of "modern art's will to silence, its hostility to literature, to narrative, to discourse. As such the grid has done its job with striking efficiency. The barrier it has lowered . . . has been almost totally successful in walling the visual arts into a realm of exclusive visuality."[20] Hence, the intrusion of science's analytic model into art has quite a different result when the defined elements are purely visual. It creates opaqueness rather than transparency, for if the grid "maps anything, it maps the surface of the painting itself."[21] Or so the modernist critics would have us believe. While there is something to this observation, especially in light of the centrality of the autonomy ideal, Krauss herself notes that Mondrian's use of the grid is complex, since he sometimes treats the grid as a self-contained extension inward from the frame edge (cf. Figure 7), while at other times he crops the edges, as in his diamond paintings, to imply an extension outward toward infinity.[22] This tension between the two ways of regarding the grid points toward a fundamental paradox within the modernist program, which, in being anti-naturalistic, attempts to deny any references to the outside. Yet it is difficult to see how the overtones of the extensive continuum can ever be removed from Western art, once they have embedded themselves into our learned modes of visualization. This is why the attempt to remove painting completely from discourse can never succeed.

Kiefer's own act of negation in *To the Supreme Being* has already shown us how the forms negated continue to reverberate within what remains, a fact that Kiefer knows how to exploit fully. The dialectical richness gained by employing such negation-gestures points toward the general textuality of all visual art, rather than toward any real possibility of either pure visuality or spirituality. Whereas the analytical tools of Classical age thinking enabled the synthesis of new forms of knowledge, the very attempt to purify art by eliminating any referential function makes such a synthesis seemingly impossible within art. Yet there is no reason we have to accept this reading of modern art, since some of its greatest practitioners, such as Henri Matisse and Pablo Picasso, retained the sense of textuality and dialectical richness, thereby enhancing their ability to command our sustained interest. Rather than our concluding that conceptual development within the arts requires preoccupation with logical processes, to the exclusion of anything else, we should conclude from these examples that truly advanced thought requires the reintegration of logical processes with those aspects of reality to which they can be applied. Kiefer's joining of the image of the grid to the image of the tree, while acknowledging his admiration for Mondrian's achievements, at the same time displays his ironic grasp of modernism's self-created double bind in trying to isolate itself from nature and from history.

The ironies multiply the more we see modernism trying to maintain itself within the exclusive visuality of painting. As Krauss has observed, the logic of the grid requires repetition, whereas the central value promoted by modern artists has been originality.[23] This emphasis on originality masks from our view the fact that the infrastructure of the grid, like the analytical structures created within the Classical age, gains its power from repeated applications, making it possible to organize art into a system. Nevertheless, a system is the very opposite of what modernists have wanted to advocate. The conflict between the artists' self-image as innovators, featuring the value of the *different,* and their use of instruments that, in effect, feature *sameness,* gives us a clear sign of what happens when art attempts to isolate itself from the rest of historical discourse. While the grid gives scientific thinking the power to define reality and to contribute materially to its cultural shaping, the net effect of the purely visual grid has been to perpetuate the idea of a purely aesthetic art, resulting in art's continuing fringe status within modern culture. In effect, this has disarmed art from achieving any effective fundamental criticism of the prevailing world view and ethos. Above anything else, we can see that a postmodernist like Kiefer rejects this outcome of the avant-garde program.

As for those modernists who treat abstract networks, to the exclusion of any other content, as essential to progress in art, Kiefer challenges them frontally by his historical allusions to pre-scientific thought. Rather than accepting an art that features detached visualization, he points toward the benefits to be gained from a reconsideration of the more fluid modes of thought involved in ancient forms of conceptualization. Thus, Kiefer offers parallels between the artist and the ancient blacksmith, as well as comparisons between the artist's transformation of materials and the alchemist's transformative operations on natural substances. In later chapters we will examine these aspects of Kiefer's approach and how they pose challenges to the dominant role science plays in shaping our conception of the visible world.

For the present, we must note another of the ironies eventuating from the modernist emphasis upon detached visuality: its reinforcement of the forms of political power dominant in the modern era. Such a claim may seem preposterous in light of the avant-garde's commitment to political protest, yet we have seen in the Introduction just how far the outcome of their efforts may be from the intentions they had. Kiefer exposes the complexity attached to the political side of art by associating the artist's palette with destructive historical forces, as in his *Nero Paints* (Figure 8). This association of the palette with fire is common in Kiefer's work. The charred landscape provides the background for a palette, floating on the air above, the tips of the brushes appearing as tips of flame that ignite the houses of the surrounding region. We have seen how *Operation "Seelöwe"* portrays the situation of collective masses in relation to imaginary planning operations, suggesting that Kiefer believes the political powers exerted by modern nations over the collective depend on imaginary forms parallel, in some respects, to the functioning of imagination within vision. As we will see later, the terms of postmodern political practice require more than defiant avant-garde gestures on the part of artists.

Kiefer seemingly questions the idea that art can gain political leverage by retreating into purely aesthetic forms. If the artistic imagination is similar in certain respects to the imagination of the generals in *Operation "Seelöwe,"* then essential reflection on political reality requires a deeper grasp of both the power of images and the way they can, in turn, shape reality. In such a context the desire for purity in art begins to look like a form of self-deception.

Even *To the Supreme Being* may turn out to have political significance once we begin to entertain this enlarged conception of representation and imagination. Although this aspect of the work may be less evident than it is in *Operation "Seelöwe,"* it becomes plainer if we compare Kiefer's monument to a dead God with his untitled work of the same year (Figure 9), seemingly based on a Nazi architectural plan (Figure 10). We find Kiefer blacking out the space at the end of the corridor in the untitled work, even as he did in *To the Supreme Being.* In this case, the white panels that admit a faint light to the interior appear high within the vaulting space, just as they were in the Nazi war memorial. The effect of this narrower, higher interior is to enclose us even more than the building in Kiefer's other painting. The place of honor in the Nazi interior was reserved for W. Hoselmann's sculpture, *German Mother,* reflecting the Nazi ideology of womanhood and motherhood, underneath the symbol of the swastika.[24] Kiefer's deliberate act of erasing these symbols, by covering over the place of honor with a black woodcut, has a direct and clear political meaning. In addition he negates the Nazis' aesthetic tastes by replacing their ornamented ceiling with the simple design of a Leonardo-like lattice. The emptying out of the Nazi memorial has the same nihilistic import as the emptying of the chamber in *To the Supreme Being.* Both paintings address, as well, larger issues about how we celebrate and memorialize those things we collectively value.

These examples make it clear that Kiefer treats all visualizations as forms of representation, whether they are abstract or include allusions to historical and physical reality. We may ask now: can any form of visualization be interpreted as other than a representation, insofar as they are *representative* of the world view and ethos from which they arise? The idea of Alberti's Window is misleading if we take this window-image as the key to understanding the concept of representation, since we have shown that the perspective window of Renaissance depiction opens to the microcosm that falls within the macrocosm, rather than into an objectively deployed space. We have seen, as well, that the mirror function of Classical age representations can only be fulfilled within the terms of the analytical network that is a conventional creation. The transparency effect, which tempts us to see it merely as the extension of the window ideal, can only be achieved with the help of a complex system of interpretation, which normally remains hidden. We now understand the difference between the grid, which enabled Leonardo and Dürer to carry out their nature studies during the Renaissance, and the grid of the Cartesian continuum, which appears to be identical with the first form of grid only because the latter grid obscures the new system of thought that was made possible by the grid and that gave it the status of the mirror of nature. Similarly, the grid of modernist abstraction differs in its use and significance from the role it played in the Classical age, even though it derives some of its import from the scientific thought created during that age.

Krauss's unmasking of the modernist grid has important implications for our grasp of postmodern developments in painting, since she exposes an assumption of the modernist program that shows its constitution from the mirror of nature idea in another respect. If we ask what serves as the foundation for the analytical activities, either in those of the Classical age thinker or in those of the modern artist, the answer we get in the first case is the knowing subject, or mind, in the second the creative mind of the artist. Krauss develops this point in several different ways, the most important of which shows why abstraction became so essential to the program of modernism: the early modernists saw "abstraction as the tool to overthrow the material realm of nature and the means of instituting a reign of pure spirit or intellect. Modern man was thought to be conceptual man, and his art must reflect with greatest accuracy his power of intellection."[25] Although twentieth-century thought exists on the other side of the divide from the Classical age, since we regard all forms of rationality as relative to their own axiom structures, it is still possible to envision our humanity as essentially involved with conceptual powers. In fact, we find that the relativity problem intensifies this tendency since we are so acutely aware of our legislative ability with respect to all interpretive schemes. Modern artists, in reacting to this cultural situation, have seen in the abstract grid their freedom to create, now that humanity has been set free of Classical age restrictions that required that representations measure up to correspondence tests.

Krauss observes that the role of the grid within our century "allows a contradiction between the values of science and those of spiritualism to maintain themselves within the consciousness of modernism, or rather its unconscious, as something repressed."[26] The creative mind embodies both possibilities, yet in its artistic function seems at odds with systematic scientific thought. Krauss believes that the whole family of ideas concerning conceptual origin, originality, and autonomy form a mythological whole that comes unstuck once we begin to examine critically the logic of repetition implicit in the grid and the set of methodical practices that go naturally with it. The alternative is to shift toward an idea of artistic practices reflecting the general modes of discourse and textuality inherent in the rest of culture. Krauss poses the question: "What does *Picasso* mean for his art—the historical personality who is its 'cause,' supplying the *meaning* for this or that figure (clown, satyr, minotaur) in his painting? Or were those meanings written long before Picasso selected them?"[27] Postmodern artists like Kiefer, in taking seriously the idea that meanings may be "written" before their selection by the artist, begin to portray the creative act as a constituting act within discourse, requiring that this act be grasped as, in some sense, reiterating elements from the past, forming their basis. Douglas Crimp strikes the right emphasis, when he observes of postmodern art: "The fiction of the creating subject gives way to the frank confiscation, quotation, excerptation, accumulation and repetition of already existing images. Notions of originality, authenticity and presence, essential to the ordered discourse of the museum, are undermined."[28] We have seen this phenomenon at work in Kiefer's painting, since the works already considered include the deployment of cultural artifacts from religious history, German political history, and the military history of World War II and excerpts and allusions to art history as well. In so doing, he destroys any clear borderline between present and past experience, requiring instead that we engage in the hermeneutic analysis of discourse and texts. We can see that this requires a fundamental reexamination of the distinction between the picture plane as window, as mirror, and as opaque surface modeling itself on its own structure.

We do not have to accept Krauss's generalization of the grid structure to every aspect of modern art to see the force of her archaeological diagnosis. There is plenty of room for quibbling about specific cases in relation to this claim, especially when we think of artists like Matisse and Picasso, whose stature requires that we give them a prominent place within modernism but whose imaginations seem too rich to be captured by this archaeological emblem. At the same time, Krauss appears to have uncovered one root of the basic tension between scientific and artistic ways of thinking. We will see that Kiefer's painting also points toward the reality of such a tension and challenges the dominant strategies that have been employed to repress it. His work, and the work of other postmodern artists, calls forth a reassessment of the roles of science and art within modern culture, including reconsideration of the idea of art as purely aesthetic.

The haunting image of the empty chamber in *To the Supreme Being* presents us with a circumscribed space that destroys our tranquility by confronting us with the emptiness that pervades our history when we have lost confidence in the value of the received traditions in Western culture. Even modernism's attempt to circumscribe the representing act poses the danger that we will lose confidence in the practices of representation and empty them of all significance within the space of self-referential abstractions. This is the nihilism inherent in modernism. Even when a Mondrian appeals to silence to open the way to something universal, his work undercuts the rich possibilities present in received texts. Postmodern painters like Kiefer have begun to reinvest artistic discourse with referential powers, but not in the service of the old ideal of visual transparency. On the contrary, they open up questions about the nature of reality and of representational systems, making it clear that the recovery of representation opens the way to the recovery as well of pre-scientific forms of thought.

Nietzsche's rhetorical question—"Do we not feel the breath of empty space?"—formulated to convey the loss of bearings that follows upon the lost conception of theistic purpose, can be applied as well to the condition of art at the end of the modernist era. It is to Kiefer's credit that he *portrays* that empty space, asking that we consider anew what has become of our idea of the real, given the way we now perceive it to be caught within our own nets of discourse.

CHAPTER TWO

The Crisis of Modernity: Reality and Hyperreality

CHAPTER ONE HAS ESTABLISHED the close link between the concepts of reality and representation within the modern world view, particularly with respect to the ideal of transparent representation fostered by scientific thought. Foucault has helped us to see that if we conceive the mind as the mirror of nature, then even if the idea of nature is altered we may be tempted to keep some features of the mirror function intact. This means that elements of Classical age thinking may linger far after its era is over. In the case of modern art this phenomenon occurs in its use of the grid, which was originally the emblem of order within nature but which now reappears as the conceptual underpinning of the creative subject. In this new guise many of the expectations associated with the Classical age grid may continue to work silently, even after artists think they have given up all indexing of images to nature. Kiefer's use of the Mondrian grid in association with the tree has the effect of exposing the continuing operation of this cultural structure. It suggests that we need to consider just how far modernism has escaped from the world view of modernity.

Thus, the transparency ideal may reemerge in a new form even when representation has been rejected. If we think of art works as arising from a clearly conceived point of origin in the creative subject, or if we appeal to a universal ground for abstract forms, the transparency ideal may reappear by making a mute appeal to rational structure. Such an approach contrasts with the ambiguity and conflicting forces that manifest themselves in ancient views of nature. The very idea of a foundation for knowledge or for art implies a starting point from a privileged position within the world. By making imaginative use of representational conventions, Kiefer's work helps us to comprehend the complexity of our appeals to reality and the crosscurrents of meaning they entail.

In the present chapter we will consider a crisis in the world view of modernity only vaguely identified before the advent of the postmodern. We will consider how the analysis of nature and history in Foucault and Jean Baudrillard helps to undermine the notion of reality as an objective totality. Both thinkers emphasize the way in which the world view of the Enlightenment, which treats nature and history alike as manifestations of objective order, has yielded in the last century or two to a more dynamic conception of reality. The result is that nature, rather than being the grounding for history, is itself historicized. In considering Kiefer's work in this context, we will see that he, too, projects his images of reality in ways that require that we consider nature and history together. This analysis will make clear the gap that separates postmodern forms of representation from their predecessors in the Classical age. In Kiefer's case we encounter a richly textured interpretation of nature and history.

A series of paintings on the theme of "Midgard" makes this feature of Kiefer's work abundantly clear. In one version, *Midgard* (Plate II), he alludes to the Edda myths in which the Nordic gods raised up Midgard ("Middle Ground") between the underworld and heaven. Kiefer depicts the earth as a stone, cast up on the shore, with no sign of purpose and no visible support. The earth–stone appears merely to be there, the genealogical descendant of some events that emerged from the sea. The scene is painted realistically, the brushstrokes are smooth, and the tone is dark and ominous. The division of the world between upper and lower domains, de-rived by Kiefer from the cosmic division described in the Jewish Kabbala,[1] as well as from the Edda myth, is symbolized by his division of the painting into a horizontally divided diptych. The narrow band of sky above the horizon of the receding sea displays nothing, whereas the dream-space of the upper region, composed of a thick impasto, looking like the surface of fired pottery, holds its place as a dense mass hovering over the sea. The neck of a serpent appears in this space, thrusting into the sky like a missile breaking into the void. Emerging from behind the horizon line, as if appearing from behind a curtain, the head of another serpent undulates its way through space.

What are we to make of this complex imagery, which makes use of referential devices to create what we could only regard as a fictional space? Within the usual terms, the diptych is scarcely coherent. There is dissonance between the upper and lower halves, the upper portion resembling the encrusted surface of some earthy place, yet its position above the horizon suggests it is of the sky or of another world. And what about the snakes? What are they doing there in the upper space? Although visual dissonance is a familiar feature in certain forms of modern art (e.g., in Francis Bacon), Kiefer's purpose seems different from the ends those other works serve. As is so often the case, Kiefer gives us the clue by inscribing a bit of text within the painting. The word "Ragnorök" appears in the upper right corner. Ragnorök refers to the cycle of existence, described in the Edda, when the gods will be attacked by their enemies. The resulting war, led by the offspring of an evil goddess, includes a confrontation between Thor and Mithgarthsorm, a giant serpent who has surrounded the earth, waiting for the Ragnorök. Thus, Kiefer is using representational practices to create the mythical space of a cosmic drama, a purpose decidedly at odds with the attempt to mirror nature as we normally understand that term. Although nature is used as a setting for the myth, the background beliefs are altered from what we expect, since we neither believe in the ancient Nordic myths nor order the history of our people in terms of battles between the gods and personifications of evil.

In order to deepen our grasp of the clash between Kiefer's use of representational images and their earlier use, let us consider another of Foucault's observations about the change that has occurred since the Classical age:

> The threshold between Classicism and modernity . . . has been definitely crossed when words ceased to intersect with representations and to provide a spontaneous grid for the knowledge of things. At the beginning of the nineteenth century, they rediscovered their ancient, enigmatic density; though not in order to restore the curve of the world which had harboured them during the Renaissance, nor in order to mingle with things in a circular system of signs.[2]

The loss of faith in a "spontaneous grid for the knowledge of things" left successive generations with the question of how to think of reality, and how to envision human experience in relation to it. Kiefer's *Midgard* dramatically displays the problematical character of these questions for our age.

Foucault makes the point in this passage that the rediscovery of the "ancient, enigmatic density" of language did not amount to a return on the part of nineteenth-century thinkers to the world view of the past. Nevertheless, they did discover something from the past that had been lost in the prematurely unified view that prevailed in the Classical age. Neither does Kiefer ask us to return to the world view of Nordic mythology, which helps to form the cultural background of his own German tradition. Nevertheless, his use of mythological material, like his use of the traditions of alchemy and ancient metal working in other paintings, suggests his dissatisfaction with the inherited view of the world we think of as distinctively modern. We must remind ourselves of what was essential to the world view of the Classical age, and of what succeeded it, to establish a context for assessing Kiefer's gestures. As Jean Baudrillard reminds us: "As late as the 17th century, Nature signified only the totality of laws founding the world's intelligibility: the guarantee of an order where men and things could exchange their meanings."[3] Yet that view of the intelligibility of the world did not survive changes occurring in the eighteenth and nineteenth centuries. The older view yielded, as Baudrillard puts it, to a view of "Nature as a potentiality of *powers* (no longer a totality of *laws*); as a primordial source of life and reality lost and recovered, repressed and liberated; and as a deed projected into an atemporal past and an ideal future. This rise is only the obverse of an event: Nature's entry into the era of its technical domination."[4] Baudrillard's closing remark points toward the primary change he attributes to a conception of nature as a collection of *powers,* but that conception of power gives primacy to human capacities set loose by rational knowledge. In contrast, Kiefer's *Midgard* undercuts the idea of intelligible powers, presenting nature instead as a setting where a *conflict* of powers, particularly those having to do with the cosmic destiny of the earth, becomes manifest. Midgard, portrayed as an abandoned stone, left to its own fate: is this perhaps Kiefer's expression of the earth's status in our age of space adventure? Although we may employ rational systems to launch our vehicles into space, it is not clear that those systems resolve the mystery of unknown powers that may await us on those journeys.

At any rate, Baudrillard's idea concerning the changed conception of nature makes it clear that we can no longer defend a notion of nature as the neutral ground toward which our knowledge is directed. Neither his view nor Kiefer's lends support to the old conception of human experience as the mirror of nature. What nature *means* at any given time may differ from what it meant earlier. When the emphasis is placed on nature's potential for serving human projects, its significance becomes distinctively different. Only the cherished idea within modernity of the coalescence of nature and history (both subject to natural law) could make it appear otherwise.

Baudrillard makes clear this close link between nature and history when he notes that our technological age seeks both to dominate nature and to treat the past in an atemporal way. The one purpose leads to the other: our desire to dominate nature requires that we neutralize the past and focus our interest on the projected future of our technical dreams. Our attitude toward time and toward our own historical activities also appears as a major theme within Kiefer's works. As we shall see later, when we turn to larger questions about mythology and alchemy within Kiefer's work, he confronts us with questions about our relation within the present to a past that still remains active in some way, and he also has a way of undermining our confident expectations about an improved future. These issues are central in Kiefer's whole work; indeed within postmodern art generally.

Our view of reality, so long as it treats the present and the future as the primary actuality, with the past appended as a mere background to present activity, lacks the richness called forth by Kiefer's representational images. If nineteenth-century thinkers rediscovered "the ancient, enigmatic density" of language, an artist like Kiefer is busy uncovering the enigmatic density of images that hark back to ancient ways of thinking long repressed. He is therefore opposed to modern tendencies to treat the past as a mere storehouse of images. The question of how the past intrudes, whether we want it to or not, is posed repeatedly in works like Kiefer's "Ways of Worldly Wisdom" series, in which he asks the viewer to ponder an intrinsic relationship joining Germans of the past into a common enterprise, thereby raising for his contemporaries the question of whether they are independent of that past. In one well-known painting (*Ways of Worldly Wisdom*, Plate III), Kiefer presents portraits of philosophers, poets, statesmen, military figures, and other leaders of German culture, which are etched into a forest background and linked together by branches that seem to form them into an organic whole. No clear line of demarcation separates nature from history in this work: nature provides the setting and the metaphor by which we may understand German history. But equally, the powers of past history inscribe themselves in the natural space. These portraits, borrowed from existing images created by earlier artists, appear around a burning log fire, which stands at the center of the composition: this raises the question of whether we are burning, or might just as well burn, the forms of worldly wisdom inherited from the past. Yet this question calls for active consideration rather than a nihilistic dismissal of the past. Contrary to a nihilistic outlook, Kiefer seems to be reiterating the position of Nietzsche's Zarathustra, who points toward our wish to be rid of the past in order that we may get on with the actions that will shape the future according to our dreams. Such an attitude is present in postwar Germany, where even references to the romantic forest setting were rejected in favor of the new world, to be created in place of the old. Yet the past remains as a limit on those projects. Here is what Zarathustra teaches:

> Will—that is what the liberator and bringer of joy is called: thus I have taught you, my friends! But now learn this as well: The will itself is still a prisoner. Willing liberates: but what is it that fastens in fetters even the liberator?
>
> "It was": that is what the will's teeth-gnashing and most lonely affliction is called. Powerless against that which has been done, the will is an angry spectator of all things past.
>
> The will cannot will backwards; that it cannot break time and time's desire—that is the will's most lonely affliction.[5]

The question, as Nietzsche sees it, is whether we are able to learn to affirm the past, as *our* history, rather than expressing angry vengeance against the past we would rather not acknowledge. Kiefer seems to be asking the same of his German contemporaries, asking them to take a new look at the past, where they may find values that are more than ancient, primitive, or underdeveloped in comparison to our own.

Nietzsche's emphasis on the will points toward the change in modernity's outlook in the last two centuries, when the Classical age ideal of the mind as the mirror of nature gradually came to be replaced by a conception of humanity's historical nature. The Classical age ideal of a convergence between natural law and history came up against the recalcitrant materials of history; conflicts of interest, shifting power relationships, and the demoralization resulting from failed ideals together contradicted the form of rationality that governed Classical age culture. Like Nietzsche's thought, Kiefer's art seems intent on confronting the self-deception inherent in the dream of a rational world, his scorched-earth paintings serving as a painful reminder of the forms of destruction our ways of worldly wisdom have so far visited on the planet.

To summarize the line of thought we have been pursuing, the shift from the Classical age view of reality to more recent forms of modernity has required the synthesis of nature with history. Where the seventeenth-century theorists could begin by assuming a fixed structure of natural law, later theorists have had to adjust their thinking to incorporate changing categories of interpretation into their idea of reality. At the same time, the counterpart to the orderly structure of nature, the mind that mirrored nature's own rationality, has been gradually replaced by the image of historical humanity, whose interpretations must suffer a measure of disorder and relativity. This implies a changed conception of both nature and history, reflected in such paintings as *Midgard*, which treats nature as a primordial source of life and historical experience as shrouded in the mythical. Similarly *Ways of Worldly Wisdom* confronts our tendency to eclipse the past by making past sources into real presences. In addition it suggests that even our conception of the forest changes radically under different historical conditions, so that in the case of postwar Germans it became emblematic of the unspeakable historical practices of the recent past. Although the world view of modernity carries with it a particular idea of the real, Kiefer's art challenges that view as too limited.

Although *Midgard* may be about the situation of the earth within the cosmos, the symbolic status of the earth raises questions about our own status as well. If we were to take seriously the idea that we have only a locally based perspective within the universe, rather than one that gives access to universal law, that would significantly alter our conception of our humanity. In *Midgard* the outside space, so full of potential threat, calls for supplementation of experience and the expansion of our imaginations. If there is no single grid by which to interpret nature, then we must find, within the residue of historical forms, a basis for our own identity. And the images we encounter, whether representational or abstract, lack universality. Like sentences within a text, which we read as falling within a larger story, the images we encounter require an imaginative placement within a larger setting, making their representational or non-representational thrust a matter for interpretation in each case. In this respect, Midgard's fate and our own are not dissimilar. Although each image presents fragments of reality for our consideration, we are not sure what proportion it bears to the whole, nor even whether there is any whole.

Such an outlook fits with the vantage point of Nietzsche, whose critique of the assumptions of modernity paves the way for developments within postmodern thought. Nietzsche defined the essential shift that must occur in postmodern thought when he attacked the distinction that enters into every discussion of truth and reality: the distinction between appearance and reality. Without this distinction, the notion of accurate representational images would never have arisen as a linchpin of Classical age thinking. The attempts of Classical age thinkers to validate representations were directed toward matching appearances against a prior, stable reality. Concerning this distinction, Nietzsche makes the following pointed claim:

To divide the world into a "real" and an "apparent" world . . . is only a suggestion of decadence—a symptom of declining life. . . . That the artist places a higher value on appearance than on reality constitutes no objection to this proposition. For "appearance" here signifies reality once more, only selected, strengthened, corrected.[6]

Nietzsche regards the artist's willingness to limit himself to fragments of the real as a healthy sign of engagement with life. Moreover, it reflects a genuinely historical point of view, since reality can only manifest itself through available perspectives and categories. Nietzsche also points out that, far from making the artist's renderings useless for understanding reality, the concrete grounding of their work in appearances has the effect of presenting "reality once more." The temporal encounter with reality through art, although bearing no guarantee as to its representative nature, nevertheless may provide meaningful perspectives that make it less likely that we will take some abstractive network as transparently real.

This issue is crucial for understanding postmodern forms of representation, since they contrast with the rejection of representational practices on the part of early modernists. The latter group often spoke as if they could penetrate the veil between appearance and reality by turning inward: away from objects and toward the expression of inner need, inner feeling, or inner thought. Yet when we substitute the image of historical humanity for the mirroring of nature by the rational mind, such an inward turn is scarcely credible. We must turn instead toward the portrait gallery of Kiefer's *Ways of Worldly Wisdom* setting, which makes use of existing images to formulate an interpretation.

We are now ready to consider another dimension of Kiefer's painting practice. As we have already observed with respect to *Operation "Seelöwe,"* Kiefer has sometimes prepared for his paintings by setting up simulated environments within his studio. In part, these are forms of visual experimentation, which have led him to create photographic books and large paintings on these themes. One of these series, the "Bilderstreit" series, arises from a studio simulation of a battle between toy tanks set within mounds of sand organized to resemble a desert plain, the tanks having been arranged in various positions around a stone tablet shaped like a palette. Kiefer assimilates the tank battles to iconoclastic controversies in the ancient church, inscribing the names of some of the ancient protagonists into the various battle positions. By implication, he assimilates them also to controversies within the contemporary art world, which is having its own battle over the status of images. In one of the paintings on this theme (*Bilderstreit*, Figure 11), Kiefer presents the image of a large palette form, serving as the central field of battle for several tanks, whose guns seem to shoot the wash of paint that drips over it. Kiefer's serious attention to historical parallels between contemporary controversies about images and those within the church in the past suggests his understanding of the strong grip images have over our view of reality. (Note the reversal of the attitude of the Classical age.) Baudrillard points out that those ancient iconoclasts, who opposed the use of images of God in any form, may have understood all too well the threat they entailed for religious belief. What threat? Baudrillard answers that they saw in the power images have the possibility that God *was* only an image.[7] He adds a moment later, "It can be seen that the iconoclasts, who are often accused of despising and denying images, were in fact the ones who accorded them their actual worth."[8] If we ask what their worth is, on this view, it is a decidedly different one from what they have been assigned within the mainstream of Western thought, where they have been treated as secondary within the appearance-reality dichotomy. Gilles Deleuze cites Plato's distinction, in Book X of *The Republic*, between images that are "on the one hand the iconic copies (likenesses), on the other the phantasmatic *simulacra* (semblances)."[9] This distinction, so central to Western thought about representation, carries over even into modernism, where the emphasis on abstractions having authentic presence reiterates the distinction between iconic copies and simulacra. But the attitude toward images in the "Bilderstreit" series, as well as the attitude toward them in the ancient iconoclastic controversies as portrayed by Baudrillard, renounces the division between likenesses and simulacra. One possibility we must now consider is: perhaps there are *only* simulacra, and the distinction between images that have likeness and those that do not concerns a relationship between two items within the realm of images. This claim goes to the heart of controversies about artistic origination, since acceptance of the generality of simulacra would imply acceptance, as well, of the textuality of all art, and an attendant grounding of all originating acts within cultural reality.

Deleuze argues, in fact, that the question of origination was involved in Plato's formulation of the distinction between icons and simulacra, falling within Plato's practice of reasoning by division. Within the "method" of division, Deleuze sees Plato as practicing "the selection of the lineage: the sorting out of claims, the distinguishing of true claimant from false."[10] What determines the true claimant, you may ask? In the case of the statesman, for example, Deleuze thinks Plato regards the true statesman as a "shepherd of men" only because he is in the lineage of the god, who is the *original* true shepherd. In contrast, the false shepherd, a mere simulacrum, is only superficially like the true one, since he does not have the proper foundation in the original. Neither does the simulacrum, painted by the painter, measure up to Plato's standard of true likeness.

Deleuze believes that Plato came close to facing up to the central issue posed by his practice of division through lineage: "Plato, by dint of inquiring in the direction of the simulacrum, discovers, in the flash of an instant as he leans over its abyss, that the simulacrum is not simply a false copy, but that it calls into question the very notion of the copy . . . and of the model."[11] Kiefer's "Bilderstreit" simulations suggest, in fact, that anything can serve as model, anything as copy, except that the distinction between true and false copy has lost its force. The disturbing analogy created by Kiefer between tank warfare and palette warfare, like the analogy he drew in *Operation "Seelöwe"* between the imaginations of the generals and those of artists, points out the dilemmas we face in a world where natural norms have been lost and where the creation of new forms of identity, through the use of whatever images may be on hand, leaves us afloat in a condition resembling Midgard's abandonment.

The question this line of reasoning poses is just how far we can push the practice of simulations and the concept of the simulacrum, which is so much at odds with our old convictions about

FIGURE 1
To the Supreme Being, 1983
Oil, acrylic, emulsion, shellac, straw, and woodcut fragments on canvas
278 × 368 cm
Musée National d'Art Moderne, Paris

FIGURES 2–3
Leonardo da Vinci, *The Last Supper*, 1495–1498
Interior of the Church of Sta. Maria delle Grazie, Milan
Courtesy of Alinari/Art Resource

FIGURE 4
Piet Mondrian—Arminius's Battle, 1976
Piet Mondrian—Hermannsschlacht
Oil on canvas
245 × 112 cm
Collection Geertjoos Visser, Belgium

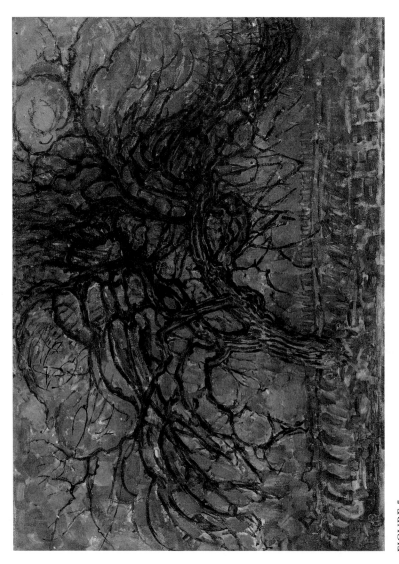

FIGURE 5
Piet Mondrian, *The Red Tree*, 1908
Oil on canvas
70 × 99 cm
Gemeentemuseum, The Hague, The Netherlands
Courtesy of Estate of Piet Mondrian/VAGA, New York

FIGURE 6
Piet Mondrian, *Trees*, c. 1912
Oil on canvas
94 × 69.8 cm
Carnegie Museum of Art, Pittsburgh
Patrons Art Fund

FIGURE 7
Piet Mondrian, *Composition 2*, 1922
Oil on canvas
55.6 × 53.4 cm
Solomon R. Guggenheim Museum, New York
Photo: Robert E. Mates

FIGURE 8
Nero Paints, 1974
Nero malt
Oil on canvas
220 × 300 cm
Collection Prinz Franz von
    Bayern, Munich

FIGURE 9
Untitled, 1983
Ohne Titel
Oil, emulsion, shellac, and straw on woodcut on canvas
260 × 190 cm
Collection Erich Marx, Berlin

FIGURE 10
Hans C. Reissinger, Consecrated Hall (*Weihehalle*) in the House of German Education,
Bayreuth, with W. Hoselmann's sculpture, *German Mother*

FIGURE 11
Bilderstreit, 1977
Oil on canvas
220 × 270 cm
Stedelijk Van Abbemuseum,
Eindhoven, The Netherlands

FIGURE 12
Aaron, 1984
Acrylic, emulsion, shellac, and
    photo scraps on photograph
65 × 83 cm
Private collection

Immanuel Kant   Joseph V. Eichendorff

Annette von Droste-Hülshoff   Martin Heidegger

FIGURE 13
The Battle of Teutoburg Forest, 1979
Die Hermanns-Schlacht
Xylographs on paper on mechanical pulp board, 66 pages bound with linen
60 × 50 × 15 cm
Private collection

FIGURE 14
Varus, 1976
Oil and acrylic on burlap
200 × 270 cm
Stedelijk Van Abbemuseum,
Eindhoven, The
Netherlands

FIGURE 15
*Ways of Worldly Wisdom
—Arminius's Battle,*
1980
*Wege der Weltweisheit—
Die Hermanns-Schlacht*
Acrylic and shellac on
woodcut
335.4 × 538.5 cm
The Art Institute,
Chicago

FIGURE 16
Ways: Sand of the Mark
Brandenburg, 1980
Wege: märkischer Sand
Acrylic, shellac, sand, and
gluten on photograph on
burlap
255 × 360 cm
Saatchi Collection, London

FIGURE 17
Painting of the Scorched Earth,
1974
Malerei der verbrannten Erde
Oil on burlap
95 × 125 cm
Private collection

reality. Baudrillard, for one, believes our elevation of the simulacrum, and our attendant indifference to the notion of the iconic copy, has gone very far indeed. In fact, he believes we have entered a new phase of civilization, which even Marxist criticism has failed to characterize properly: the mirror of nature has been superseded by the mirror of production: "Abstraction today is no longer that of the map, the double, the mirror or the concept. Simulation is no longer that of a territory, a referential being or a substance. It is the generation by models of a real without origin or reality: a hyperreal." [12] His idea is that our civilization has begun to organize itself around the production of hyperreal entities, reflecting the coding processes we have invented. Like the genetic code, which establishes a pattern in miniature antecedent to the reality that develops from it, Baudrillard holds that "the real is produced from miniaturised units, from matrices, memory banks and command models —and with these it can be reproduced an indefinite number of times. It no longer has to be rational, since it is no longer measured against some ideal or negative instance. It is nothing more than operational." [13] Baudrillard's historical diagnosis is that this state of affairs reflects the total triumph of the ideal of production within our history, so that productive activity no longer needs any justification based on anything outside itself. The production models simply *are*, and they are able to produce and reproduce whatever society is able to consume.

Baudrillard's analysis goes far toward shaping the terms of discussion that we must have about contemporary art. Since many recent artists have identified with the neo-avant-garde, keeping alive the protests that were central to earlier avant-garde movements, we need to compare their approach with that of other postmodern artists, like Kiefer, who do not subscribe to the neo-avant-garde program. In part the debate concerns the uses to which representational elements are to be put: will it be to ironically mimic operational production, as in Andy Warhol's Campbell soup paintings, or will it be to establish references to the plight of the earth and to our own fate, as in Kiefer's *Midgard*? While these uses do not necessarily conflict, we recognize a totally different spirit at work in these polar extremes of postmodern practice. Baudrillard sets the terms for the discussion because he underlines the way humanity has changed from the reflective being of the Classical age, who shaped activities within standards set by nature, to the productive being, who has learned to "*posit himself* according to this scheme of production which is assigned to him as the ultimate dimension of value and meaning." He adds that through "this *mirror* of production the human species comes to consciousness [*la prise de conscience*] *in the imaginary*."[14]

But that means that Nietzsche's elimination of the appearance-reality distinction might foreshadow our energetic creation of the hyperreal, producing and reproducing things, and formulating and reformulating images, without purpose or grounding beyond the productive activity itself. In this way, we might view the Bilderstreit simulations as generating Bilderstreit photographs and Bilderstreit paintings without end, with no more reason for their production than their expression of the genetic flow from the structure from which they began. Origination understood as simulations according to a code: is this the new idea of creativity to be drawn from postmodern art?

In Kiefer's case, such an account of creativity seems a poor fit with his actual practices, which seem designed to counteract that attitude toward images exposed by Baudrillard's analysis. This suggests that, just as Baudrillard perceives the ancient iconoclasts as genuine defenders of the importance of images, we perceive Kiefer as reviving that attitude within his Bilderstreit studies. Because images are downgraded in late capitalist society to a merely instrumental use within production and consumption, as is evident when we remember how advertising uses images only to create desires for products, there may be some need for contemporary artists to offer updated iconoclastic protests to affirm their own sense of the other uses images may have.

This is a particularly compelling aspect of contemporary debates about postmodern art, since some critics have reacted negatively to Kiefer's art because they have seen him as betraying the avant-garde program. In assessing this criticism, we must ask whether Warhol's ironic imitations of production imagery—whether of Campbell soup cans, movie stars, or political figures—

undermine or reinforce those cultural practices. Do his serial repetitions of images, directed against their bourgeois manifestation,
serve a revolutionary purpose or contribute additionally to those
practices? We recall again Peter Bürger's view (discussed in the
Introduction) that the historical avant-garde movements suffered
absorption into the institutions they sought to overthrow, and we
noted, as well, Bürger's view that the neo-avant-garde had failed to
learn that lesson. In his analysis of the situation, Bürger pointedly
criticizes the defenders of the avant-garde ideal for championing
the value of the new, reminding them of the fact that novelty,
or at least the appearance of novelty, resides at the center of the
value system of commodity production.[15] Bürger's judgment on
the neo-avant-garde is equally harsh:

> The painting of 100 Campbell soup cans contains resistance to the
> commodity society only for the person who wants to see it there. The
> Neo-avant-garde, which stages for a second time the avant-gardiste
> break with tradition, becomes a manifestation that is void of sense
> and that permits the positing of any meaning whatever.[16]

Since Bürger's judgment in this matter seems sound, we must
ask where we might find an effective critical challenge to the world
view spawned within the Classical age and modified into the production culture since the nineteenth century. In answering this
question, we must remember that the defenders of a purely aesthetic art have conformed with the terms of Baudrillard's diagnosis
that through the "*mirror* of production the human species comes to
consciousness *in the imaginary*." This makes it clear how akin the
ideals of creativity and production are.

The irony of history here is no different for the avant-garde
than it is for Karl Marx himself if Baudrillard is correct. Baudrillard thinks that, even though Marx exposed the myths of capitalism and undermined its attempt to associate economy with natural
law, he was guilty of embracing capitalism's central value when he
placed labor at the center of his scheme. What Baudrillard believes
Marx failed to see is that it is not just the *content* of capitalist productive activity that must be critiqued, but also the *form* production
itself—that is, production treated as a central value. Therefore,

"Marx did not subject the *form production* to a radical analysis any more than he did the *form representation*." [17] Baudrillard therefore thinks that Marx's critique, focused as it was on the origin of exchange value, failed to reach the diagnostic center of the capitalist value system. Similarly, Bürger's critique of avant-garde art points to the failure of the avant-garde, and even more of the neo-avant-garde, to be radical enough in their critique of bourgeois values. Although their negation of academic art was in reaction to the idea of representation in the Classical age, they may not have fully comprehended the idea of representation that had taken its place, surreptitiously, in industrial society. That is why they failed to grasp that their emphasis upon artistic means, *as* means, was perfectly in accord with the role of technique in the Industrial age. Baudrillard adds, as well:

> It is a new generation of signs and objects which comes with the Industrial revolution. Signs without the tradition of caste, ones that will never have known any binding restrictions. . . . The problem of their uniqueness, or their origin, is no longer a matter of concern; their origin is technique, and the only sense they possess is in the dimension of the industrial simulacrum.
>
> Which is to say the series, and even the possibility of two or of *n* identical objects. The relation between them is no longer that of an original to its counterfeit . . . but equivalence, indifference. In a series objects become undefined simulacra one of the other. [18]

The question in this historical context is whether any art can pose a challenge to this dominance of technique, this tendency toward seriality, and the inexorable drift toward equivalence of value. The shift toward the simulacrum might have the effect of producing indifference toward anything except momentary value.

The issues here are complex, but Kiefer's portrayal of the war of images, his treatment of German heroes in *Ways of Worldly Wisdom*, and his use of ancient myths to confront our thoughtless preconceptions, all raise possibilities of criticism that address the heart of industrial civilization's problems. In doing so, he invests his images with supports falling outside the equivalency arena of industrial simulacra. What sort of grounding does he give them? This question is wrongly put if we expect a return to the notion of grounding that representational images had within the Classical age, since our analysis has demonstrated the way that form of support has been superseded. Deleuze's analysis puts the point in just the right way, because we have had to face up to the loss of the distinction between iconic copy and simulacrum. Thus, when I speak of Kiefer's resisting the equivalency valuation that images receive in Industrial society, it is not in order to reject the simulacrum problem. On the contrary, Kiefer's attitude, expressed through his own simulation practices, is that we can borrow resources from any place, yet not randomly or indifferently; their original value may still have a role to play. This means that he is able to make use of historical materials and mythological perspectives to help confront the limitations of our own way of thinking.

Many commentators on the development of postmodern art have pointed out how much at odds it is with the ideals of Enlightenment thought, which have shaped the civilization of the Industrial age. In part, this is because of the resistance of no less a social critic than Jürgen Habermas to postmodern developments. The reason for his opposition is his perception that the Enlightenment project of remaking history needs to be completed, whereas postmodern thinkers like Foucault are skeptical about the continuing relevance of that project of modernity.[19] Modernist art falls within that dream of an improved history, with many of the modernist practitioners having regarded their use of abstraction as a sign of progress in art. This is the reason for the opposition on the part of some modernist critics to Kiefer's work, since they see his use of archaic materials, his attitude toward the past, and his use of representational conventions as rejections of modernist ideology.

How are we to understand this feature of Kiefer's work, and what light does it shed on postmodern art in general? Baudrillard helps us to understand this feature of postmodernism through the emphasis he places on the role of the productivity *model* in the capitalist political economy. This is where he sees Marxism sharing the values of capitalism. He argues:

> Radical in its logical analysis of capital, Marxist theory nonetheless maintains an *anthropological* consensus with the options of Western rationalism in its definitive form acquired in eighteenth century bour-

geois thought. Science, technique, progress, history—in these ideas we have an entire civilization that comprehends itself as producing its own development and takes its dialectical force toward completing humanity in terms of totality and happiness. Nor did Marx invent the concepts of genesis, development, and finality. He changed nothing basic: nothing regarding the idea of man producing himself in his infinite determination, and continually surpassing himself toward his own end.[20]

Baudrillard's belief is that this feature of modernity is contradictory to the social form of archaic and primitive societies, where ideas of exchange and reciprocity are much more at the center of social life. He argues that the exchange idea of modern society, which depends on the individual producer and the individual consumer, controlled by the exchange values of production, contrasts sharply with societies founded on the idea of symbolic exchange. In the latter case, personal needs and personal use are not in the picture. Because of this, Baudrillard says that the "*symbolic must never be confused with the psychological*. The symbolic sets up a relation of exchange in which the respective positions cannot be autonomized."[21] The implication concerning autonomy points directly to one way the ideology of modern art is, like Marxist anthropology, caught within the net of the ideology of political economy.

As Baudrillard has so persuasively argued, the mode of being of most earlier societies entailed a form of symbolic exchange that placed them in more intimate concourse with nature, which means that "part of the harvest will immediately be returned as firstfruits in the process of sacrifice and consumption. . . . Above all, it must never be interrupted because nothing is ever taken from nature without being returned to it."[22] We can see a similar attitude expressed in Kiefer's *Midgard* and in other works in which he makes use of the exchanges between the alchemist and nature and between the blacksmith and nature. And the reciprocity ideal of archaic societies seems to be reiterated, as well, in his "Ways of Worldly Wisdom" portraits of figures from German history. If a relationship of sharing were substituted for the idea of historically surpassing our ancestors, new forms of identification would be possible for contemporary humanity.

Within the ideal of productive humanity, the autonomous individual becomes the focus of any self-identification, whereas identifications within archaic societies have much more to do with the cycle of existence and the destiny of the tribe, the city-state, or the village. That is why Baudrillard thinks it an error for Marxist interpreters to treat the ancient master-slave relationship, for example, as a relationship between two autonomous subjects, since that form of subjectivity is the product of later historical developments.[23] The question of personal autonomy, understood in psychological terms, is also challenged in the "Ways of Worldly Wisdom" series. Here the self-identification question posed by Kiefer for himself and for his German contemporaries falls within symbolic, rather than psychological, terms. This makes sense in relationship to Baudrillard's observation that, "in the primitive exchange gift, the status of goods that circulate is close to language. The goods are neither produced nor consumed as values. Their function is the continuous articulation of the exchange."[24] If we think of language functions as the best example of reciprocal exchange, where everyone who speaks contributes to the creation of the language, then an alternative to modernist autonomy models for creation begins to take form.

In reviewing the direction our analysis has taken in this chapter, we can now see that the return to the use of representational images within postmodern painting is not, as some critics have charged, a simple reversion to the past. On the contrary, it is clear in Kiefer's case that we are confronted with challenges to the modern world view, taking the form of alternatives to our understanding of both nature and history. With respect to both concepts, Kiefer's work appears to portray a cyclical view of existence rather than one organized according to the causal and linear time structures characteristic since the Classical age. We will return to this theme in later chapters. *Midgard* also displays Kiefer's concern that we need to ponder our place within the larger cosmos, even though our technical brilliance tempts us to think that our codes of rational structure, by which we create hyperreality, make the consideration of such questions a manifestation of outmoded thought patterns.

The question of how we are related to the past, within the

terms of this changed situation, is of the utmost importance, for it would appear that if there are only simulacra, the old cosmic questions no longer have any relevance. Baudrillard also poses a challenge to Kiefer's use of the past when he suggests that nostalgia is the great temptation when "the real is no longer what it used to be."[25] If Kiefer escapes the nostalgia trap, he only does so by falling back on an ontology like Heidegger's, which portrays the world in more elemental terms than those found in modern thought. Heidegger recognizes that a simpler view of reality, and of history, was involved in pre-scientific forms of thought. He argues that we should reconsider our world view by thinking of the world in terms of four elemental categories: the earth, the sky, divinities, and mortals.[26] What Heidegger intends is that we regain our sense of elemental location within the world, where the dome of the sky opens above the earth, revealing that which *is* in terms of unfolding events within this space. These events have everything to do with human mortality, and the mortality of those things that we find within nature and that we ourselves create. They also reflect the hopes, ideals, and cycles of existence associated in the past with divinities, promising as they do a continuing history of mortal creations. Although we must consider how the meaning of historical creations gets altered within a world understood in terms of simulacra, lacking the background of divine purpose, it is enough for the present to note the way Kiefer's Midgard symbolism seems to require a shift in ontology, making the status of humanity within both the cosmos and history questionable. In raising such questions, his work exposes us to forces in the world that modern humans had learned to ignore.

CHAPTER THREE

Original Representation: Theater of Cruelty Painting

T HE FIRST TWO CHAPTERS have analyzed the change that occurred from the Classical age to the present in our conceptions of nature, representation, and human experience. Whereas nature had been conceived as an orderly whole governed by natural law, and reason as the capacity to mirror nature, the more recent period treats nature as a collection of powers awaiting transformation by humans. Yet our technological and industrial projects leave many features of the older view intact, especially those having to do with the acquisition of knowledge. In many respects we vacillate between paying deference to nature and projecting our own desires onto reality. The removal of natural norms leaves a vacant niche, which the humanist outlook fills in by giving free rein to the interpreter or creator. Modernism's emphasis upon originality is one sign of this state of affairs.

However, when an interpreter like Baudrillard exacts the price to be paid by this outlook, even raising doubts about our idea of the real, we begin to wonder whether there may be some alternative more satisfactory than immersing ourselves in the play of the simulacra. If there is no more basis for creations and actions than the individual agent, then the humanist outlook appears to be in great jeopardy. A gradual erosion of confidence in this outlook raises questions about what to say about the fragmentary character of experience and of the reflexive circle of our historical actions.

The alternative lies in the direction of reassessing the setting within which experience and action arise. In part this means considering anew those traditions that modern thought has discarded, and also, perhaps, reconceiving the place of humanity within the cosmos. We have seen that Kiefer's *Midgard* provokes questions about whether the forces at work in the cosmos provide any support for human purposes and values. In order to confront these questions, Kiefer presents us with images that bring us back to discarded traditions and point toward an elemental relationship to nature that modern scientific thought has cast aside.

Such issues come to the surface through works like Kiefer's *Johannisnacht* (Plate IV), one of his collages in which three erect fern fronds appear in the foreground, reaching like dancers into the sky, whose movement celebrates the festival of Midsummer's Night. But these dancing nature forms appear before another erect figure, photographed and overpainted in black, appearing through a "window" in the blackened space. This second scene reveals an industrial pylon, creating a tension between the nature forms and an image of technological reality. At the same time, this work establishes a conflict between our expectations of originality and the reproductive media, since the photographic base of the work is a repeatable image like those that appear in news and travel magazines. This is a characteristic feature of many of Kiefer's works of the 1980s. In addition, because the fern forms are cutouts pasted onto the surface, *Johannisnacht* sets up a counterpoint between photographed image, cutout forms, and a painted surface that says nothing in its own right, leaving us in doubt about what is original and what reproduced. This dissonance in Kiefer's work challenges modernist assumptions and indicates his postmodern understanding of the nature of signs. It also establishes tension between the representation of natural forms and the productive activities of industrial civilization.

Other complicating factors appear in Kiefer's work. For example, the circular form above the central fern cutout reminds us both of the midsummer sun and of an image in *Aaron* (Figure 12), one of Kiefer's other works, where a single fern reaches toward a circle above, serving as a metaphor for the relationship Moses and Aaron had with Jahweh. In *Aaron* the fern evokes memories of the rod Aaron employed in leading the Exodus. These reverberating strands point toward an intertextual basis for the images, giving Kiefer's work a measure of convergence with other developments in postmodern thought. He mixes imagery from several different domains in many of his works (e.g., images from nature festivals with biblical texts, nature symbols with technological references, mythological with historical motifs, and signs of war and destruction with symbols of regeneration and hope). Either these conflicting images represent a form of eclectic confusion or they reflect a deliberate strategy on his part to separate his work from the aesthetic strategies of modernism. In the present chapter, I will argue that Kiefer's return to representational practices deliberately points toward an intertextual basis for images and helps to create a new form of representation. Jacques Derrida refers to this as "original representation,"[1] a term he invented to describe the form of representation Artaud created through his Theater of Cruelty.

Artaud wanted his theater to expose conflicting forces that manifest themselves in reality but that get overshadowed by our ideas of rational order. Artaud envisioned a form of theater that puts aside mimetic representation in favor of an encounter with elemental forces. He says that the "theater still remains the most active and efficient *site of passage* for those immense analogical disturbances in which ideas are arrested in flight at some point in their transmutation into the abstract."[2] Kiefer's *Johannisnacht* is one such site, as is his *Midgard*. In the present chapter we will consider how Kiefer's work introduces *original representation* into art by comparing his visualizations to Artaud's ideas about the Theater of Cruelty. We will consider, as well, the way this exposure of conflicts compares with certain aspects of ancient tragedy.

If we return to Kiefer's *Midgard*, we can begin to develop these ideas. One reason for the painting's power is the compelling sense of abandonment it expresses. If the earth is to be regarded as a lonely stone, surrounded by unknown forces that constantly threaten it, our idea of reality must undergo a fundamental alteration. Rather than reflecting any sort of pre-existing purpose, reality begins to appear as Nietzsche characterized the universe:

> a monster of energy, without beginning, without end; a firm iron magnitude of force that does not grow bigger or smaller, that does not expend itself but only transforms itself; as a whole, of unalterable size, a household without expenses or losses, but likewise without increase or income; enclosed by "nothingness" as by a boundary.[3]

He adds a little later that the world is "a sea of forces flowing and rushing together, eternally changing, eternally flooding back."[4]

We might react to Nietzsche's sketch by celebrating the way it liberates human potential, thereby extending the Enlightenment's humanistic ideal. Thus, we could regard the elimination of outside purposes as opening the way to human creativity, making it possible to turn enthusiastically toward the creation of "hyperreal" forms, freed from the reality principle taken for granted in Classical age thought. However, Kiefer's paintings undermine this easy optimism by confronting us with symbols of forces that modern rationalism has put aside. The snake in *Midgard* alludes to the kind of forces that threaten to undermine our projects and dreams. In another version of *Midgard* (Plate VI), Kiefer portrays the earth-stone as a broken palette (a device previously employed in his Bilderstreit simulations); it appears in the center of the painting in counterpoint with another large serpent, slithering its way into the palette's cracks. This association suggests that even art must come to terms with such forces, thereby undermining the innocent basis for creativity envisioned among many modern artists.

How are we to understand this side of Kiefer's art, and what does it show us about his shift away from the modernist ideology? An easy (but wrong) answer would be to dismiss Kiefer as just another pessimist. When he paints the scorched earth, he typically turns those images of despair into overdetermined images, which also project renewal and hope within the same space. In one of these paintings, *Cherubim, Seraphim* (Plate VII), the landscape is black, looking as if it were covered by flowing lava, into which he has inscribed two white stones (labeled, respectively, "Cherubim" and "Seraphim"). They refer to two members of the celestial hierarchy described by the ancient writer Dionysius the Areopagite.[5] They are inspired by Kiefer's encounter with two gigantic white stones on a barren stretch of landscape in Yugoslavia.[6] By placing these stones within the context of the scorched earth, Kiefer affirms the possibility of renewal even in the face of human destruction. These symbols of hope counteract the painting's tendency to remind us only of the effects of war or environmental disaster, real or imagined. Although Kiefer's work seems to distance him from the easy optimism of Enlightenment thought, he nevertheless often tempers tragic presentations with such symbols of hope and renewal.

In the Introduction we noted Kuspit's idea that contemporary German painters use referential conventions to establish a fictional framework, rather than for purposes of realistic reference. This is certainly true of Kiefer, whose Midgard paintings are *stagings* of ancient myths, designed to confront us with troubling questions about our own time. In a similar manner, the white stones of *Cherubim, Seraphim* are staged symbols, which enable Kiefer to expose an elemental conflict for interpreters of twentieth-century history. This is true not only of the black/white conflict but also of Kiefer's appeal to ancient religious mythology in the context of twentieth-century historical practices.

Such dramatic staging devices occur in many of Kiefer's other paintings. A particularly striking example is the series of wooden rooms that Kiefer painted early in his career. One of the most powerful of these, *Parsifal II* (Plate VIII), alludes to Wagner's music-drama. Kiefer presents us with a space at once realistic and abstract. Although the massive beams and the wall framing the space make it appear that we can enter the empty attic room, the painting resists our desire to read it in simple realistic terms. Kiefer quite clearly shows us the conflict between his "realistic" depiction of the attic space and the practices of modernist painting. He flaunts his ability to paint in the modernist way by his handling of the woodgrain motif, which he almost turns into a play of abstract forms; by his texturing of the surface through alternating smooth brushwork with techniques that give it material presence; and by the sheer size of the work, which reminds us of the abstract sublime. Nevertheless, his practices are postmodern, since his slashing of the beam in the right foreground makes evident that his painterly gestures are mixed with collage-like elements, suggesting perhaps the reproduction of the image within a context bearing all the signs of an original.

His practices remind us of Walter Benjamin's analysis of the changed conditions of artistic creation in an age of mechanical reproduction.[7] Kiefer's works reflect an implicit recognition of these changes, since he makes frequent use of photographs, prints, and other reproductive media within his paintings. Benjamin envisions the displacement of the painter's contemplative stance by the camera's penetration into reality, resulting in a more fragmentary encounter with the world. Kiefer's mixed-media presentations appear to reflect such a perception, thereby challenging modernism's ideal of the purity of the medium and its aura of originality.

Moreover, he employs conventions of Renaissance perspective, but in ways that alter their effect. For example, the perspective created in *Parsifal* gives an exaggerated size to the beams, creating the feeling that we are below the floor level looking up onto a stage. This provides a theatrical atmosphere, heightened by the bowl set in the center of the room, which is positioned like an altar and filled with blood, evoking memories of blood sacrifice and other archaic forms of human expression. Over the bowl, Kiefer has inscribed the words "Höchsten Heiles Wunder! Erlösung dem Erlöser!" ("Miracle of the highest salvation! Redemption to the Redeemer!").[8] These features create a symbolic conflict that we are left to resolve, raising the question of whether the Parsifal ideal, the music-drama that celebrated it, and the culture that supported them both has played a positive or negative role within history.

What is the purpose of this *staging,* which is by no means unusual in Kiefer's work? Why does he make it deliberately theatrical? In answering this question, we must turn to Artaud's Theater of Cruelty rather than toward the mimetic theater. Jacques Derrida points out that Artaud wanted to challenge in a fundamental way the classical theater of the West, which he regarded as "theological" theater, one that operated from "the groundwork of a pre-established text, a table written by a God-Author who is the sole wielder of the primal word. A theater in which a master disposes of the stolen speech which only his slaves—his directors and actors —may make use of."[9] Derrida's understanding of Artaud's practice is that Artaud wanted to eliminate the distant dominance of the author, who controlled the stage through the text as God was supposed to control the world by his plan of creation, and whose representatives (directors and actors) were to express "the content of his thoughts, his intentions, his ideas."[10] In addition, he wanted to eliminate the passivity of the audience, who become mere spectators when they seek to view the author's intentions represented by the actors. The Theater of Cruelty involves, therefore, rejection of the classical model of representation, even as Derrida wishes to question, in general, the idea of representation as iconic copy.

Artaud puts forth the idea that the theater needs to move away from purely aesthetic goals, which he regards as symptomatic of a refusal by modern culture to confront unpleasant realities. In contrast, archaic cultures found it necessary to examine them:

> The old totemism of animals, stones, objects capable of discharging thunderbolts, costumes impregnated with bestial essences—everything, in short, that might determine, disclose, and direct the secret forces of the universe—is for us a dead thing, from which we derive nothing but static and aesthetic profit, the profit of an audience, not of an actor.
>
> Yet totemism is an actor, for it moves, and has been created in behalf of actors; all true culture relies upon the barbaric and primitive means of totemism whose savage, i.e., entirely spontaneous, life I wish to worship.[11]

Artaud wants to bring the theater alive to the working of elemental forces, instead of continuing a theater oriented toward the creation of aesthetic distance. He perceives that modern culture has learned to insulate itself from active engagement with life, thereby making the theater into a place that, like the museum, is only for remembering a dead past. In contrast, Artaud advocates the following idea of an authentic culture:

> To our disinterested and inert idea of art an authentic culture opposes a violently egoistic and magical, i.e., *interested* idea. For the Mexicans seek contact with the *Manas,* forces latent in every form, unreleased by contemplation of the forms for themselves, but springing to life by magic identification with these forms. And the old Totems are there to hasten the communication.[12]

Artaud wants to create the Theater of Cruelty in order to realize such a "magic identification" with elemental forces. He refuses to accept a theater limited either to entertainment or to aesthetic contemplation. One feels that Kiefer also uses the imagery of the Midgard paintings to affect such an identification, even as he does with the bowl of blood in *Parsifal.*

Artaud also speaks favorably about the Balinese theater, which foreshadows the Theater of Cruelty idea by putting aside exclusive emphasis on the goals of the author, featuring instead the director as "a kind of manager of magic, a master of sacred ceremonies. And the material on which he works, the themes he brings to throbbing life are derived not from him but from the gods. They come, it seems, from elemental interconnections of Nature which a double Spirit has fostered."[13] This means that the goal of theater is directed more toward the active engagement of the actors and the audience with the drama, even as the goal of any ritual is the active involvement of the participants in the ritual process. Kiefer's use of provocative symbolism seems designed in the same way to evoke active responses from his viewers.

Artaud's dream of such a theater has its roots in an understanding of art that goes back to Nietzsche, who argued:

> Almost everything we call "higher culture" is based on the spiritualization and intensification of *cruelty*—this is my proposition; the "wild beast" has not been laid to rest at all, it lives, it flourishes, it has merely become—deified. That which constitutes the painful voluptuousness of tragedy is cruelty; that which produces a pleasing effect in so-called tragic pity, indeed fundamentally in everything sublime up to the highest and most refined thrills of metaphysics, derives its sweetness solely from the ingredient of cruelty mixed in with it.[14]

What Nietzsche means is that the primitive and barbarian forms of cruelty have undergone change over history, transforming themselves into sublimated forms of expression constituting higher culture. In the case of Greek tragedy, Nietzsche believed that the Greeks had found a way to express and to contemplate negative factors embedded in the world they encountered.

Nietzsche created the categories "Apollinian" and "Dionysian" to describe how this was so within Greek tragedy. What they drew from the tradition of Apollo and the other gods of Mount Olympus was the power of dreams and clear images to inspire beautiful plastic illusions.[15] Rather than decrying this orientation toward the dream world, Nietzsche regards it as an essential feature of the high achievements of Greek culture, making it possible for them to strive for the perfection of form we have come to associate with their art, particularly with their sculpture. At the same time, Nietzsche argues that the Greek spirit drew upon another tradition, the Dionysian, which expressed their understanding of the power and destructive potential that all life forces have when their earthly demands intrude into our dreams, distorting their purpose and making them into something illusory. For example, although the ideal beauty of a Helen could inspire the Greek spirit with dreams of beauty and splendor, the destruction produced under the influence of that ideal in the Trojan Wars did violence to those dreams and exposed their limitations. The tension between such conflicting forces appears in Kiefer's juxtaposition of the white celestial stones with the blackened landscape in *Cherubim, Seraphim.* According to Nietzsche, the tradition of the Dionysian celebrants responded to deep cosmic energies, understood in both positive and negative terms by the Greeks. Within the drama, he thinks that the main story line expresses the Apollinian vision, while the Dionysian forces appear within the deep structure of the drama, often conveyed through the music and rhythm of the chorus. It is within the Dionysian aspect of the drama that such values as cruelty are manifested, and these conflict with the more refined vision of a civilized society.[16] Nietzsche believed, therefore, that Greek drama gained its power from the juxtaposition of these seemingly incompatible poles of human existence.

The vantage point of Apollinian vision can only be maintained by an act of aesthetic distancing, which isolates the space of the art works from reality. But reality never quite conforms to the visions of civilized people. In the Greek case the ideal vision appears through Olympian religion and Homeric culture, but they conflict with the older nature religions of the region. These religions nevertheless continued to hold a considerable fascination for the Greeks, even though they contained elements that were primitive by the standards of the later civilization. For the citizens of Athens the intensity of feeling and participation with nature from the older tradition continued to exert an attraction. Although the Titan gods had been displaced by the Olympian deities, they expressed an aspect of the human condition that the dramas continued to address.

Nietzsche speaks of ancient tragedy as an exercise in cruelty because it undermines the self-image Greek citizens sought to maintain. Thus, Nietzsche sets up the contrast between the Dionysian image of man, symbolized by the satyr, and the image through which the civilized citizen viewed himself:

> Nature, as yet unchanged by knowledge, with the bolts of culture still unbroken—that is what the Greek saw in his satyr who nevertheless was not a mere ape. On the contrary, the satyr was the archetype of man, the embodiment of his highest and most intense emotions, the ecstatic reveler enraptured by the proximity of his god, the sympathetic companion in whom the suffering of the god is repeated, one who proclaims wisdom from the very heart of nature, a symbol of the sexual omnipotence of nature which the Greeks used to contemplate with reverent wonder.
>
> The satyr was something sublime and divine: thus he had to appear to the painfully broken vision of Dionysian man. The contrived shepherd in his dress-ups would have offended him: on the unconcealed and vigorously magnificent characters of nature, his eye rested with sublime satisfaction; here the true human being was disclosed, the bearded satyr jubilating to his god. Confronted with him, the man of culture shriveled into a mendacious caricature.[17]

This ancient theater of cruelty is just what Artaud seems to want and what Kiefer appears to emulate in many of his works. While the Parsifal myth appeals to the higher ideals of bourgeois humanity, making the quest for the holy grail a journey of piety and heroic grandeur, Kiefer's relocation of the myth within the confines of an empty attic room appears both to revere the myth and to debunk its pretentiousness. Moreover, its association with the spilling of blood raises the question of whether its historical effect has been what civilized humanity had intended. Kiefer's Dionysian sensibilities locate an element of self-deception in the historical Germans' enticement by such myths, thereby confronting his contemporaries with the question of whether the future they desire may contain similar tendencies toward self-deception. His allusions to the cruelty and barbarity manifested in the past make it clear that we must do more than commemorate human history: we must criticize it as well.

This line of reasoning accords well with Derrida's conception of original representation, which takes us back to the elemental connection we have to the world, with no higher form of representation really ever being able to separate us from Dionysian desire. Dionysian art celebrates such a relationship of human to world by reestablishing the close connection ancient people had to it. As Derrida sees Artaud's idea of this:

> [The stage] will not even offer the presentation of a present, if present signifies that which is maintained *in front* of me. Cruel representation must permeate me. And nonrepresentation is, thus, original representation, if representation signifies, also, the unfolding of a volume, a multidimensional milieu, an experience which produces its own space. *Spacing [espacement],* that is to say, the production of a space that no speech could condense or comprehend (since speech primarily presupposes this spacing), thereby appeals to a time that is no longer that of so-called phonic linearity, appeals to a "new notion of space" and "a specific idea of time." [18]

The attempt to have Dionysian reality "permeate me" means that the total effect of the staging must take priority over any momentary presence it might create. Unlike the modernist emphasis on authentic presence, the Theater of Cruelty creates a complex space in which that which is happening requires a response that stimulates ongoing interpretation. This is evident in the case of Kiefer's *To the Supreme Being,* considered in Chapter One. That is one reason original representation links to the idea of different levels of textual interpretation. The complex levels of interpretation at work in *Cherubim, Seraphim* and in *Parsifal II* make this abundantly clear. The scorched earth of *Cherubim, Seraphim,* which evokes memories of destruction of the landscape by world war bombings or anticipations of nuclear holocaust, contrasts in ambiguous ways with the heavenly stones, whose white color and apparent purity seem to project hope and inspiration. Yet the uneasy tension in which these elements exist creates a space set apart from normal representation: it is the space of original representation.

Although Derrida speaks here of "a new notion of space," it is not readily evident what exactly that entails. He says that it is the "production of space that no speech could condense or comprehend." In part that is because the vantage point in paintings like *Cherubim, Seraphim* and *Operation "Seelöwe"* is inconsistent. It requires that we struggle to unify what cannot be read within a single interpretation. Such is the case in *Johannisnacht*, which requires that we arrive at a vantage point concerning nature that unifies nature as a collection of Dionysian powers with nature as giving rise to productive powers through its predictability. The space within which this conflict occurs is radically at odds with the uniform space of Classical age conceptions of reality and with its role in industrial production.

At the close of Chapter Two we considered the alternative ontology Heidegger advocates in opposition to the modern conception of reality. He argues that we should return to an elemental ontology built around the ideas of earth, sky, divinities, and mortals. The terms of the Theater of Cruelty seem closer to that ontology than they do to the ontological structures that govern modern "realism." Heidegger holds, in fact, that if we were to recapture our sense of nearness to things, we would see them in a new light. Accordingly, our idea of space would be altered from the matrix of objective relationships to something nearer to ourselves. Thinking of a bridge over the Rhine, for example, differs from thinking of an object within scientific space. Heidegger argues:

> [From] this spot right here, we are there at the bridge—we are by no means at some representational content in our consciousness. From right here we may even be much nearer to that bridge and to what it makes room for than someone who uses it daily as an indifferent river crossing. Spaces, and with them space as such, . . . are always provided for already within the stay of mortals. Spaces open up by the fact that they are let into the dwelling of man.[19]

And it is central to Heidegger's idea about art that art can open up reality by bringing us nearer to things. Although Heidegger offers a more complex understanding of representation than one that plots a content against an objective background, Derrida charges that he retains "the truth of unveiled presence" as his guiding idea about art.[20] In contrast "the new notion of space" that Derrida associates with the Theater of Cruelty rejects any vestige of the idea of unveiled presence. We can understand Derrida's position if we turn to Kiefer's *Midgard* and *Cherubim, Seraphim* as visual examples. His treatment of the horizon line in these paintings (typical of so many of his landscapes) turns the difference between earth and heaven into a sign-difference between the visible and the invisible. Gudrun Inboden, whose excellent article on Kiefer appears in the Paul Maenz catalog, has described this aspect of Kiefer's landscapes as follows:

> Earth and heaven make up the protagonists; the horizon takes care of casting the parts. And yet, nothing is happening. The plowed fields are fallow; heaven is pushed back, pushed almost out of the pictures. There is nothing to cushion the missing event: Neither fog nor light, nor any other natural phenomenon between heaven and earth allegorically replaces the incident. The infinitely vast horizons . . . do not lead us to the atmosphere of the infinite. They are the boundary between heaven and earth: Instead of melting "near" with "far," they separate that below from that above.[21]

This emphasis upon the horizon as boundary locates Kiefer's spacing act just where Derrida would think is appropriate: elemental differences (earth/heavens, below/above, near/far, visible/invisible) are the subject matter of original representation, and we never approach the condition of *unveiled* presence—that is, a form of presence where we get behind or beyond such differences to the naked things. The idea of nature as providing normative structures violates the rudimentary functioning of sign-differences in experience and interpretation. Benjamin helps to point in this direction in formulating his argument that the camera changes human sensibilities because of the way the equipment penetrates into reality. "Evidently a different nature opens itself to the camera than opens to the naked eye."[22] By thus making reality relative to our sign systems and technologies, Benjamin anticipates the emphasis Derrida puts upon the differentiating acts that enter into every aspect of experience.

Derrida finds the original condition of sign-representation particularly at work within language, where sound stands in contrast to silence, where punctuation and the space between the letters and words are as necessary as the letters and words themselves, and where meaning (as unveiled) is always deferred. This constant deferring indicates "the specific idea of time" that Derrida associates with the spacing act of the interpreter. The use of signs involves an irreducible temporalizing act, since even the ordinary idea of signs implies that "signs represent the present in its absence; they take the place of the present. When we cannot take hold of or show the thing, let us say the present, the being-present, when the present does not present itself, then we signify, we go through the detour of signs."[23] Derrida ultimately questions whether there is really any detour, which explains why he thinks that Heidegger is mistaken in not ridding himself of all vestiges of unveiled presence (e.g., by retaining the idea of the naked thing to which we may draw near). Derrida holds instead:

> Difference is what makes the movement of signification possible only if each element that is said to be "present," appearing on the stage of presence, is related to something other than itself but retains the mark of a past element and already lets itself be hollowed out by the mark of its relation to a future element. This trace relates no less to what is called the future than to what is called the past, and it constitutes what is called the present by this very relation to what it is not.[24]

This general point about the nature of signs appears to be reflected in Kiefer's handling of various visual signs within his art. Not only is this true of his staging of the landscapes, but we see it as well in *Parsifal II*, where his staging of the myth and of the Wagnerian use of it confronts his contemporaries with questions about how those traces shape their own present and future. Thus, Derrida's point about *differance* is as much a perception about how values function as about linguistic and other sign systems. Modernity's idea that rationality can function in the present with the past safely distanced from it comes under frontal attack.

With these implications of the Theater of Cruelty clarified, we can see how they are related to Nietzsche's understanding of ancient tragedy. According to this line of reasoning, tragedy gains its force from its power to confront, to challenge, and to undermine forms of established "civilized" value, where hidden agendas and unexpected outcomes distort their intended purposes. Its effectiveness is likely to be enhanced where there is already a conflict within the heart of a people's values. J.-P. Vernant has observed with respect to Greek tragedy that it arose just when there was an unresolved conflict between the older, heroic culture and the new conception of the city-state, governed by law:

> The tragic turning point thus occurs when a gap develops at the heart of social experience. It is wide enough for the oppositions between legal and political thought on the one hand and the mythical and heroic traditions, on the other, to stand out quite clearly. Yet it is narrow enough for the conflict in values still to be a painful one and for the clash to continue to take place. A similar situation obtains with regard to the problems of human responsibility that arise as a hesitant progress is made towards the establishment of law. The tragic consciousness of responsibility appears when the human and divine levels are sufficiently distinct for them to be opposed while still appearing to be inseparable.[25]

Although the situation of conflict stems from other factors for a contemporary practitioner of the tragic arts, many of the same elements are present. What are the contemporary conflicts that provide the basis for a Theater of Cruelty? In the case of Kiefer, the Midgard series depends in part upon a conflict between the ambitions of contemporary humans to explore the cosmos and the fear of unknown forces that may govern beyond the earth. In this situation, the ancient traditions of the Nordic gods have relevance to contemporary concerns, even if we treat the stories as mere myths. The symbolic force the ancient myths have for us arises from their expression of uncertainty and dependency in the face of unknown powers. But how can such concerns occur in an age of science and technology, since we venture into space through the systematic knowledge and precise techniques that express the central values of our age? As Baudrillard has argued, we have great faith in the simulation sequences that enable us to achieve our purposes, where the codes invented in electronic systems, computer networks, and statistical packages govern the unfolding of events in predictable ways. Yet the fact remains that, despite the confidence we feel in such systems, Kiefer's Midgard depictions catch us for the moment without any defense, intrigued by the image of the naked stone representing the earth, whose fate still determines our own no matter what our simulation programs may promise.

Thus, although our conflict is not between the city-state's self-rule by law versus governance by the gods, the ingredients in the contemporary conflict are not so different from the ancient conflict as they may at first appear. The two poles of the conflict for the ancient Greeks had to do with the predictability and rationality of their own system of law, on the one hand, and the unpredictability and lack of rationality that seemed to govern the older, heroic culture, on the other. Although the terms of our situation are not precisely the same, the symbolic role of the sea, which still destroys the things created by our technological ingenuity, appears in Kiefer's Midgard paintings to remind us of the *limit* that intrudes into our design for the future.

Nor is the question of tragic conflict confined to the relationship between nature and human projects, since Kiefer also locates the conflicts within historical tradition itself. He displays keen sensitivity toward the way collective goals create results that fall outside control by individual action. One allusion to this factor is the depiction by Kiefer of the situation of mass wars in such paintings as *Operation "Seelöwe."* Here the mass action of the troops, seemingly expressing the will of the three absent generals, falls outside the modes of behavior we normally associate with life within the community. Moreover, Kiefer's sense of the complex relationship we have to the past, symbolized by the branches of the trees in *Ways of Worldly Wisdom*, which bind together the heroes of past German culture, generates the same question: how far does individual responsibility extend, given the intricate relationships we have to the past? This sense of the strong grip the past has over present realities occurs, also, when Kiefer makes metaphoric use of trees and woodgrains to express both the way the history of the growth of trees and human history remain actively a part of the reality of present life. These appear especially in books of woodcut studies on the Battle of Teutoburg Forest (Die Hermanns-Schlacht). One example (Figure 13) shows the heads of Martin Heidegger and Immanuel Kant within the woodgrain motif; in one version they appear on facing pages, alluding both to the philosophical derivation of one thinker's ideas from the other and to the way both enter into our own thought, even as the inner layers of the tree help form the substance of the outer layers. Kiefer employs the woodgrain in a similar way in the Parsifal painting considered above (Plate VIII), where the woodgrain of the attic floor alludes to the symbolic role Wagner's music-drama gave to that myth in recent German history. Similarly, the Hermanns-Schlacht theme, which refers to the ancient victory of the German general Hermann over the Roman general Varus, becomes a basis for Kiefer's continuing presentation of the German past to his contemporaries. In one large painting on this theme, *Varus* (Figure 14) Kiefer creates a forest scene where the trees surround a snow-covered path punctuated by spots of blood, onto which he inscribes the names of the main protagonists. The arching branches of the trees display the names of other characters from German history.

The sense of tragic conflict, therefore, is not confined to a conflict between human purposes and cosmic forces, since it is just as much a part of Vernant's sense of the tragic, and of Nietzsche's too, that there should be a conflict between contemporary people and their past culture. The collective background, expressing itself in any people's history, is one feature of the Dionysian side of tragedy. Vernant especially emphasizes that the Dionysian religion was a collective phenomenon, but one falling outside the practices of the official city-state religion. Kiefer's paintings display, as well, the conflict between one collective phenomenon and others that form the conscious center of a culture. If *Varus* refers to a heroic episode, championed by the mainstream of German culture, this patriotic identification contrasts with collective entanglements that have led to bloodshed and, ultimately, in the case of Germany, to the Holocaust. Although many Germans did not approve of the radical measures taken by their leaders, one outcome of collective action may be like the one expressed through Dionysian religion, where the festival itself helped to create collective behavior unthinkable within the setting of the more civilized city-state religion. Vernant speaks of the sense of personal fusion with the divine in Dionysian religion. He adds:

> Dionysus is a master of magic and illusion; a god of wonders, perplexing and disconcerting, never where he is nor what he is, essentially elusive, the only one of all the Greek deities, it has been said, that no form could embody, no definition encompass because, both within man and in nature, he embodies what is radically other.[26]

It is this feature of the human condition that the Theater of Cruelty is designed to expose, since it seeks to deconstruct the hidden sources of cultural identity that will never surface in the usual theater setting. Below the level of conscious comprehension, the Dionysian element continues to work, even though it is elusive and enigmatic. Nevertheless, it is there.

The task of tragic art is to make it evident and to bring the conflict to the surface. As Vernant puts the point, the spectator is then in the position to perceive what the characters, living through their situation, can never quite see:

> The language becomes transparent and the tragic message gets across to him only provided he makes the discovery that words, values, men themselves are ambiguous, that the universe is one of conflict; only if he relinquishes his earlier convictions, accepts a problematical vision of the world and, through the dramatic spectacle, himself acquires a tragic consciousness.[27]

The tragic consciousness consists of the realization that humanity is not able to deny the Dionysian aspect of its nature, except at the price of self-deception. A central reason for the tragic presentation therefore, is to help us overcome such self-deception, exposing us to the underbelly of our own historical consciousness. No small portion of Kiefer's *oeuvre* satisfies this purpose.

The implications for art itself are as important, for our purposes, as seeing what Kiefer himself is doing. In other words, the concept of personal identity, the importance of which has already been discussed for the modernist paradigm, is implicated in this discussion of tragic consciousness. If the creation of art depends upon the will of the artist, then the question of the status of the will is of the utmost importance in assessing the modernist ideology. We must exercise care here, since this question has far-reaching significance for other aspects of our discussion. Nietzsche made the observation: "Willing seems to me to be above all something *complicated,* something that is a unity only as a word."[28] What he means is that there is no simple unity of consciousness to form the basis for an act of will, whether on the part of an ordinary human or on the part of the creative artist. Rather, he argues that every act of willing involves a complex of feelings, of the development of those feelings over time, and of thought and emotion as well. The *plurality* of aspects composing a seemingly simple act gives more room for confusion and self-deception to flourish than it does for clarity of intention.[29] This is especially pertinent to our discussion of tragic consciousness, since Vernant makes the claim that, within the context of the ancient tragedy, a criminal act may have a complex origin, incommensurable with our notion of responsible action. He says:

> The action does not emanate from the agent as from its source; rather it envelops him and carries him away, swallowing him up in a power that must perforce be beyond him since it extends, both spatially and temporally, far beyond his own person. The agent is caught in the action. He is not its author; he remains included in it. Within such a framework there can clearly be no question of individual will. The distinction between what is intentional and what is enforced in the action of the subject does not even make sense here. How could one, of one's own volition, be misled by error? And once it has been committed how could the misdeed-defilement possibly not carry its punishment within itself, quite independent of the intentions of the subject?[30]

Vernant's understanding is that complex causality is *always* a part of the setting for actions within tragedy, since the actors always know only a part of what they need to know to avoid the tragic outcome. Therefore, they are in the position of being unable, in principle, to take what modern society defines as fully responsible action. In this regard, our judgment must be that their actions are more like those of the insane, whose lack of knowledge or lack of control leads us to excuse them from responsibility for what they do. Yet a simple judgment excusing the actions misses part of the thrust of this historical-tragic sense of action.

To develop this point further, we must note that one of the intentions of Artaud's Theater of Cruelty was to release the shadow that lies behind every image. By this Artaud meant to release a kind of magic that is central in primitive ideas of causality, but that modern notions of causality and action have put aside. Artaud says: "Like all magic cultures expressed by appropriate hieroglyphs, the true theater has its shadows too." In contrast, our "petrified idea of the theater is connected with our petrified idea of a culture without shadows, where, no matter which way it turns, our mind [*esprit*] encounters only emptiness, though space is full."[31] Artaud wanted to release the hidden shadows, which a theater structured according to the ordinary idea of personal causality could not achieve. In pointing toward a double causality within ancient tragedy, Vernant appears to be reasoning along the same lines. He argues that the actions of the tragic figure appear to require two kinds of explanation, if we are to comprehend what goes on within the drama: one having to do with the person's individual character and the *ethos* that governs the culture, the other having to do with the gods and the person's *daimon*.[32] This makes it essential that we see that "the logic of tragedy consists in 'operating on both planes,' in shifting from one meaning to the other, always—to be sure—conscious of the opposition between them but never rejecting either."[33] In the ordinary theater the *daimon* layer of significance lies hidden, whereas in the Theater of Cruelty Artaud wishes to release it.

And, as we have seen in this chapter, so does Kiefer in his painting practice. The way in which he utilizes historical references to invoke a complex background of causality creates ambiguous images, whose overdetermined meaning leaves us groping. Rather than our being able to fall back on any Classical age conception of the unity of reality, we find ourselves baffled by partly mythological, partly realistic pictures, which use abstraction to some other end than to express the projections of a creative subject. One gets the feeling that Kiefer is groping in the shadows, seeking to release the questions that hover in the background, unsure himself of what they may reveal for those who have the courage to allow them to do their work. The palette of the Midgard painting, cracked and broken on the ground, symbolizes the broken dream of modernist creativity, which sought to shift the basis for art away from material reality and toward the purity of spiritual vision. Kiefer shows us, however, that purity of vision is the last thing we should aspire to, caught as we are within the sign differences that constitute our experience. By creating his own Theater of Cruelty, Kiefer exposes us to questions about our understanding of history, the causality of actions, and the direction in which our dreams may be carrying us. In moving from the privileged representation of the Classical age to original representation, Kiefer helps us to see that we must reassess the nature of human action and consider anew our conception of history.

PART

II

*The Artist's Texts
and Cultural
Dissemination*

Part I has established the difference between Classical age ideas of representation, which were governed by the ideal of transparent meaning, and the contemporary idea of original representation, which denies all forms of transparency and asserts multiple meanings that require ongoing interpretation. Whereas the Classical age view of reality presupposed an ordered objective totality whose counterpart was the rational conscious subject, the idea of original representation expresses lack of confidence in such a whole and locates human experience within conflicting levels and forces. This means that we must reconceive the nature of the human subject. Rather than grounding experience within the privacy of the mind, the idea of original representation locates experience within cultural reality and within a people's encounter with elemental forces.

It concerns an original relationship to actuality, prior to any separation of the mental act from that which it represents. Accordingly, human experience unfolds in terms of symbolic exchanges between humans and nature and within community activities. That is why Baudrillard warns, in a passage quoted in Chapter Two, that the "symbolic must never be confused with the psychological." Prior to the idea of grounding experience in the psychological subject, human experience unfolded in terms of using and interpreting signs, marking and being marked, and creating communal activities and ritual celebrations expressing responses to locally based actualities. Nothing was transparent since symbolic meaning is always overdetermined. Although cosmological concerns were often expressed, they occurred without the bias toward totality that governs modern metaphysical thought. Since Kiefer's work returns us to the context of symbolic exchange, we must now consider what it would mean if we were to put aside a psychologically based idea of creation and interpretation. This question is central to Part II.

We have already seen, with the help of Rosalind Krauss, that modernism has retained many of the assumptions of the Classical age view of reality and of the human subject. Her deconstruction of the modernist's use of the grid has revealed the centrality of the conceptual subject in creating modern works. We need, therefore, to explore what it means to shift from thinking of art works as originating from the individual subject to thinking of them as appropriations of existing texts and symbolic forms. Whereas modernism conceives artists as expressing individual perspectives through their work, postmodern thought conceives artists as having to achieve personal identity through the play of textual interpretations. Part II analyzes how the shift to a textual basis for art affects our understanding of creativity, history, and cultural memory. Kiefer's works help to open up these issues by the way he employs cosmological, mythical, and historical narratives to challenge our preconceptions about humanity and the world.

CHAPTER FOUR

The Death of the Subject
and the Birth of the Text

I N T H E C O N C L U D I N G S E C T I O N of Chapter Three, we
began to consider what is essential to a postmodern view of
the creative act. Vernant's idea that tragic action reflects different "reality" levels, arising from diverse representations of the
everyday and the daimonic, points toward a more complex idea
of actions than we find in modern humanistic thought. We have
observed the play between different domains in Kiefer's art. This
is especially evident in a work like *Operation "Seelöwe"* (Plate I),
where Kiefer visualizes two planes of reality that intersect but do
not coincide. Whether we treat the transparent platform above as
the domain of the gods or as symbolizing absent military leaders,
whose power derives from a collective ideology, it seems to sketch
a place for forces beyond the ordinary. Such representations, which
are by no means unusual in Kiefer's work, leave us wondering
from what vantage point they arise. By representing conflicting
planes of existence and by drawing from diverse cultural sources,
Kiefer undermines the central assumption of modernism: the sin-
gular vantage point of the creative subject.

It is not just that Kiefer's art confirms Nietzsche's contention
that "willing seems to be above all something *complicated*," but also
that he displays how various modes of representation enter into
our self-identity. Like other conceptual artists, Kiefer is dubious
about modernism's reliance on immediate visual presence and on
the conscious subject whose outlook it expresses. By intruding daimonic and collective elements into his depiction of reality, Kiefer
indicates a more complex view of the creator and of the art work
than we find within modernism. Victor Burgin summarizes a cen-

tral aspect of the postmodernist's challenge to modernism and its humanistic outlook:

> The common-sense view, the one which just seems *obvious,* is that we are each born into the world as a little "self" which is just as much simply *there* psychologically as it is physiologically—a little seed of individuality which over time sprouts to form the adult subject we eventually become; but psychoanalysis has built up a different picture: we become what we are only through our encounter, while growing up, with the multitude of representations of what we *may* become— the various positions that society allocates to us. There is no essential self which precedes the social *construction* of the self through the agency of representations.[1]

Burgin's point can readily be associated with Kiefer, whose work is filled with a variety of historical and mythological motifs that seem to highlight the substantive role representations have in the formation of the self. The effect is to locate questions of identity within the play of various texts, which we must integrate for ourselves. For him the tension between representing himself as German and representing himself in more general terms as an artist and as a human being is one important strand of conflict. By bringing such issues to the surface, Kiefer displays his desire to help us confront similar conflicts in ourselves. In the present chapter we will consider how Kiefer's intertextual approach alters our understanding of the creative subject and challenges ideas central to humanism.

Kiefer's *Ways of Worldly Wisdom* (Plate III) is as good a place to start as any, since his reproduction of portraits from other sources produces a museum of images requiring active interpretation on the part of the viewer. Moreover, this work creates a dissonance between different picture genres, since the nature imagery implies one genre while the frescoes of historical figures suggest another. Although the branches or vines provide a measure of visual unity, as does the fire burning at the center, the overall scene reverberates with different levels of meaning. This fact becomes even more evident when Kiefer transfers the theme to other applications, as he does in the mixed-media version entitled *Ways of Worldly Wisdom— Arminius's Battle* (Figure 15). We recall the books of prints Kiefer did on this theme, the images having been borrowed from pictures in dictionaries and books on the Third Reich.[2] Now he appropriates them for another use, taking his own prints, cutting them apart, and reorganizing them into a collage surrounding a woodcut image of forest and fire. He overpaints this picture gallery with a spider's web of branches or vines, so that the lines appear to unify the separate pictures into a whole. And yet this unifying device intrudes into each image to violate its integrity. This complex practice calls for further analysis. What is Kiefer trying to achieve through these devices?

Frederic Jameson has argued that a central feature of postmodern art is what he calls the "death of the subject." Here is how he describes this phenomenon:

> We need to introduce a new piece into this puzzle, which may help explain why classical modernism is a thing of the past and why postmodernism should have taken its place. This new component is what is generally called the "death of the subject" or, to say it in more conventional language, the end of individualism as such. The great modernisms were . . . predicated on the invention of a personal, private style, as unmistakable as your fingerprint, as incomparable as your own body. But this means that the modernist aesthetic is in some way organically linked to the conception of a unique self and private identity, a unique personality and individuality, which can be expected to generate its own unique vision of the world and to forge its own unique, unmistakable style.[3]

A number of related issues raised by Jameson are exemplified in Kiefer's handling of the "Ways of Worldly Wisdom" theme. For one thing the vantage point expressed calls attention more to the way a collection of signs interacts than to origination from a unique perspective. Kiefer borrows freely from German cultural icons, reproduces them, mixes them in various combinations, and introduces verbal labels into pictorial space. The modernist desire for pure pictorial presence is thereby violated, as is the status it gave to painting over the various reproductive media.

Like Warhol and Rauschenberg, in his "Ways of Worldly Wisdom" series Kiefer indicates his understanding of the role of images and signs within experience. Although Rosalind Krauss credits Picasso with having created "the first instance within the pictorial arts of anything like a systematic exploration of the conditions of representability entailed by the sign,"[4] Picasso remained essentially within the tradition of modern painting, where visual presence takes priority over other considerations. Kiefer, on the other hand, gives explicit priority to signs and to texts, making it clear in cases like Figure 15 that viewers must engage in a sort of archaeological dig to create their own interpretation. In "Ways of Worldly Wisdom" German cultural history is the subject, while in other works it is fascism that comes under Kiefer's probing lens. In a recent interview, reported by Stephen Henry Madoff in *Art News*, Kiefer explained:

> My thinking is vertical, and one of the levels was fascism. But I see all these levels. I tell stories in my pictures to show what's *behind* the story. I make a hole and go through. I use perspective to draw the viewer in like a bee to the flower. But then I want the viewer to get by that, to go down through the sediment, so to speak, and get to the essence.[5]

This journey "down through the sediment" requires viewers to open themselves to conflicting historical and symbolic possibilities, which may well remain unresolved. As with the psychoanalytic client, a clearly delineated identity may be lacking, requiring interpretive effort on the viewer's part.

This accords well with Jameson's idea of the death of the subject, by which he seems to mean an end to what Michael Fried saw as essential when he called Edouard Manet the first modernist painter because he was "the first painter for whom consciousness itself is the great subject of his art."[6] Fried links this emphasis on consciousness with the artist's self-conscious shaping of the picture surface. He sees the artist's own autonomy as the source of the autonomy of art works. However, "The Ways of Worldly Wisdom" reflects another approach, which Jameson describes as the "*decentring* of that formerly centred subject or psyche"[7] essential to the bourgeois idea of the individual. At the same time it reflects Burgin's description of the postmodern subject, who is "a precipitate of the very symbolic order of which the humanist subject supposed itself to be the master."[8] Autonomous mastery is the last thing suggested by Kiefer's depictions.

The status accorded to the conscious subject within humanism has already been challenged by Nietzsche, who says:

> We could think, feel, will, and remember, and we could also "act" in every sense of the word, and yet none of all this would have to "enter our consciousness" (as one says metaphorically). The whole of life would be possible without, as it were, seeing itself in a mirror.[9]

The individualism governing so much of modern thought comes under attack here, since Nietzsche holds that part of what consciousness conceals is its own derivation from a collective setting. What we fail to see within the circle of consciousness is the historical involvement we have with these collective forces. Nietzsche adds that consciousness is "only a net of communication between human beings," and is proportionate to the "capacity for communication."[10]

Kiefer is expert at drawing forth the silent collective background in unexpected ways. For example, his *Ways: Sand of the Mark Brandenburg* (Figure 16) makes use of a landscape setting to create an overdetermined historical image. The apparently neutral natural setting gets charged with emotional overtones by referring to a place in Brandenburg that has been the scene of numerous territorial struggles in the past. In addition, it spontaneously calls forth an old patriotic song, "Märkischer Heide, märkischer Sand," which was adopted as a marching song by Hitler's army. This painting operates, therefore, on a number of levels simultaneously. On the first reality level, the landscape is photographed and overpainted with acrylic and sand. Photographic reality exists in tension with painted surface, as it does with the verbal information inscribed on the surface. In addition, the literal presence of earthy material (sand) contrasts with the depiction of reality through the photograph. But most of all, nature is a prop for historical issues, the landscape reverberating with the strains of marching songs and scenes of battle in German history. Rather than modern thought's treatment of nature as the structural source for the mind's knowledge of reality, Kiefer seems to use nature as a setting invested with historical significance.

In another version of the March Sand theme, *Icarus—Sand of the Mark Brandenburg*, a palette form with a wing flies over the landscape. Kiefer's vantage point on the artist's situation is instructive in this context, since the flying palette frequently appears in his paintings as a symbol of the artist's vista. We have already considered another such example, *Nero Paints* (Figure 8), and there are several others as well. It is clear that Kiefer considers the artist's judgment of events as crucial to his role. Because of this "the palette lives high above the land where it can, in effect, look, depict, measure, interpret, and transform."[11] And yet the landscape itself indicates the earthbound condition of the artist, who is never able to achieve detached contemplation of what he depicts. One sign of this earthbound condition is his use of sand and straw as materials in several of his works of the 1980s.

Kiefer consistently creates this kind of tension between two planes of existence, between which the artist presumably must move. This may be one reason why his landscapes give the impression, as Mark Rosenthal has observed, of our "being both close to and above the ground at once."[12] Kiefer seems to see the artist as a visionary, whose outlook is both above the scene and simultaneously embedded in its historical setting. Perhaps he thinks we never can achieve the judgmental detachment necessary for total mastery of our history.

In other respects, Kiefer's work reflects a conviction that experience has multiple dimensions. A particularly fascinating example is his 1985 collage entitled *Yggdrasil* (Plate V). In *Yggdrasil* the lower portion of the work again begins from a photographic image, where a tree appears in front of a factory, a row of towers carrying power lines, and a road leading indefinitely into the distance. This plane of everyday reality yields above to an overpainted black space onto which molten lead has been poured. This lead blob moves downward to touch the treetop, and the tree appears to have been ignited by the hot lead. These elements do not seem to fit easily together. Two lines of investigation are required to comprehend them, the first of which leads us from the title, *Yggdrasil*, to the role of that name in Nordic mythology. It is the name of the tree of life (the *axis mundi*), which, according to the tale, is under threat from dragons and serpents feeding on its roots below. It is protected by three norns (fates), who repair it daily, and this activity is overseen by the gods.[13] Kiefer's collage reverberates with these overtones of threat to the tree, and one layer of meaning it has attaches to this mythological background. We will consider this issue further in Chapter Six. For the present, the other line of investigation points to the role of the poured lead in Kiefer's works of this period, when he used this material in the "Exodus" series as an ambiguous symbol for the pillars of cloud and fire by which Jahweh guided the Israelites out of Egypt. And it refers also to the ancient practices of the alchemists, who transformed materials like lead under the inspiration of a spiritual vision. Kiefer appears, therefore, to join together everyday reality with the daimonic, a natural setting with historical practices, and the present with a collective background.

The effect is to raise questions about the outlook of modern humanism, which portrays the human subject as capable of gaining control over all these factors through conscious rationality. Modern rationalism wants to deny the daimonic and to expose the collective to the negating power of individual action. *Yggdrasil*, in contrast, recalls us to the elemental power of the daimonic, of the collective, and of the earth itself. Although the intruding lead blob appears to enter from another world, it is the very material of the earth itself, transformed according to the alchemists' designs. The vantage point expressed through *Yggdrasil* is full of ambiguity and conflict, playing between the different texts to which it makes reference. Even artists are caught within this play of the texts, since their attempts to soar above the landscape to evaluate what lies below require that, like the alchemists, they transform the earth's own materials and express the historical visions that are already at hand.

We remember Kiefer's desire to lead us "down through the sediment." Examples like *Yggdrasil* undermine the picture of human thought and expression that has governed modern art. Whereas modern thought portrays itself according to the ideal of what

Nietzsche called "the daylight of reason,"[14] the daimonic, the collective, and the earthbound character of thought makes that ideal unrealistic. Nietzsche, in fact, held that the philosopher's glorification of reason reflects a lack of *historical* sense.[15] Although modern art has seemingly been outside the rationalist tradition, Krauss's analysis of the operation of the grid suggests that the image of the creative subject in art has been modeled after the cognitive subject. In place of "the daylight of reason" we get what we might call "the daylight of pictorial presence." We have already seen how Kiefer's sensitivity to representational complexity undermines any such notion.

A particularly telling aspect of Kiefer's artistic practice speaks to this issue. Leo Steinberg has argued that an artist like Rauschenberg, with whom Kiefer shares much in common, has moved away from giving privilege to the upright visual plane, turning instead to what Steinberg calls the "flatbed picture plane," a term he bases on the flatbed printing press.[16] Rauschenberg's complex overlapping images, many of which are reproduced from existing cultural images, create a sense of ambiguity for the viewer. In this respect they are similar to Kiefer's images, particularly in works like *Yggdrasil* and *Ways of Worldly Wisdom*. Steinberg goes on to say:

> Rauschenberg's picture plane had to become a surface to which anything reachable-thinkable would adhere. It had to be whatever a billboard or dashboard is, and everything a projection screen is, with further affinities for anything that is flat and worked over—palimpsest, canceled plate, printer's proof, trial blank, chart, map, aerial view. Any flat documentary surface that tabulates information is a relevant analogue of his picture plane—radically different from the transparent projection plane with its optical correspondence to man's visual field.[17]

The flatbed concerns the plane of action, rather than a purely visual plane; it is any kind of surface on which the artist "tabulates information" or produces transformations. Kiefer's collages, in particular, seem to be such work surfaces. The subject who was supposed to stand behind the modernist picture surface is now transformed into an artist in the world, working and reworking surfaces to produce images whose significance is complex, as is a text.

Steinberg's analysis converges with ideas of Burgin and Jameson, discussed earlier in the chapter, when he writes:

> Rauschenberg's work surface stood for the mind itself—dump, reservoir, switching center, abundant with concrete references freely associated as in an internal monologue—the outward symbol of the mind as a running transformer of the external world, constantly ingesting incoming unprocessed data to be mapped in an overcharged field.[18]

Kiefer's work surface, similarly, seems to portray the mind of the artist as "abundant with concrete references" and as "a running transformer of the external world," rather than as something confined to its own intentional space.

In developing this idea it is useful to consider artistic thinking in the way Rudolf Arnheim does in his study of Picasso's *Guernica*. Arnheim's analysis raises doubts about whether Picasso ever fit into the kind of modernist paradigm developed by critics like Fried and Greenberg. Arnheim argues that Picasso's work expresses what he calls "the visionary attitude,"[19] by which he means an attitude toward reality that carries out thinking via concrete visual contents. According to this view, visual thinking may operate simultaneously at several reality levels. On one level Picasso had to think of the events that occurred in the bombing of Guernica, the level on which journalists must think about depicting reality. Yet Arnheim shows that in considering the *meaning* of the bombing of Guernica for himself Picasso had to go deeper. His meditation on Guernica carried him into layers of symbolic meaning that show us that all such journalistic accounts are superficial. Picasso's final mural depicts Guernica in richly symbolic ways. It locates the deep structures of historical experience, reflecting concerns about Picasso's own Spanish heritage as well as mythological themes that reach far back into Western history. Thus, the bull and the horse, both of which play a central role in the drama of the bullfight, also possess overtones of mythological meaning that reach back to ancient culture. Picasso's own fascination with the minotaur image manifests itself again in his symbolic rendering of the import of the annihilation of that Spanish village. For our present purposes we need to observe that several levels of images interact in his mural. The final product reflects Picasso's resolution of a number of competing possibilities for understanding what Guernica means to him. Arnheim's notion of visual thinking is of something that has a complex, concrete logic that operates simultaneously on different levels. It reflects both Picasso's own history as an artist (making it possible, for example, for him to redeploy Cubist strategies within his "realistic" depiction of the scene) and the historical symbols from which he draws. In this respect, we might say with Nietzsche that genuinely historical thinking is far removed from any idea of "the daylight of reason."

The visionary attitude extends also to artists' consideration of their own role *qua* artist. Arnheim holds that Picasso identifies himself with the bull,[20] whose eyes seem to comprehend the responses to the tragedy by the other figures but whose head turns away from what he sees, suggesting that his perception creates too much pain. Yet in symboling his own role through the bull, Picasso seems to accept responsibility for making visible what such forms of destruction may mean. Similarly, we have seen how Kiefer's symbol of the flying palette points toward a parallel task for the artist.

In addition to works already considered, Kiefer's *Painting of the Scorched Earth* (Figure 17) indicates his understanding of visionary thinking. In this painting he superimposes the palette on a tree in the foreground of a landscape. A fire, burning the branch that shows through the open center of the palette, suggests that art may both destroy and purify. Like the Promethean artist of the "Sturm und Drang" tradition in German culture, the artist runs the risk of carrying fire to the earth. This imagery derives also from the agricultural practices of the region in which Kiefer lives, where the grain fields are burned over at the end of the season in order to make the land fallow before the next season's planting.[21] Thus, an apparently destructive manifestation of fire turns into a form of cultivation. Kiefer's association of the artist with fire, particularly with the alchemist's fire, indicates his strong conviction that the artist has transforming powers. Working from the real conditions of nature and history, the visionary thinker must rework and refine received meanings.

Nietzsche's desire to avoid the illusions of the "daylight of reason" are, therefore, similar to those that govern Kiefer's artistic practice. In developing these considerations it is useful to explore Nietzsche's line of reasoning further. Not only does Nietzsche raise doubts about the capacity of thinkers to detach themselves from the collective background, but he also believes that reasoning cannot be separated from passionate desires. In fact, Nietzsche holds that the philosopher's desire to understand reality as something given is illusory, since "nothing is 'given' as real except our world of desires and passions, that we can rise or sink to no other 'reality' than the reality of our drives—for thinking is only the relationship of these drives to one another."[22] The most vexing part of the thinker's quest is that reality is only accessible *through* our drives, among which we must count the drive for verbalization and the drive for visualization. Therefore, the thinker's quest for understanding cannot be completed because the thinker's own intoxication with language or images creates more instances of language and image. In the same way, questions simply generate more questions.

This approach shows what is at stake in Nietzsche's charge that the modern conception of the conscious subject is superficial. He wants to undercut the sharp distinctions we draw between the affective and the rational, and between thought and imagination. Nietzsche reinterprets the psyche as "a fluctuation of intensity,"[23] portraying experience as a flow of pulsations moving in different directions and forming themselves into different patterns. Some of them double back upon themselves to form reflective consciousness. Thus, the rational may be seen as a set of structures emerging from fluctuations of energy rather than as a separate power. That is why Nietzsche speaks of thinking as a *relationship* between drives and intensive moments.

Nietzsche's philosophy of mind, therefore, is consistent with Kiefer's notion of the sedimented layers of meaning we need to probe. If the intensive moments of experience organize themselves into different levels and patterns, then the attainment of understanding has to do with achieving ordered relationships from among these intensive moments. Chaotic thinking is unproductive just because it produces a weak, confused response to the conditions one is pondering. Nietzsche sees effective thinking as emerging from the sensual and linguistic materials that present themselves in fragmentary form within momentary experiences. Yet these moments are never self-contained since they constitute the historical flow of a person's experience.

This way of approaching thinking converges with the idea that artists practice concrete visionary thinking. This is evident in a case like Kiefer's *Shulamith* (Plate IX), in which he creates a haunting image concerning the Jewish question within German history. *Shulamith* symbolizes a Jewish woman referred to in the *Song of Solomon*, and Kiefer treats the figure in several works, placing her in counterpoint with the German heroine Margarete. Kiefer has been influenced by Paul Celan's poem dealing with this theme. A few of Celan's lines follow:

> Black milk of daybreak we drink you at night
> we drink you at noon death comes as a master from Germany
> we drink you at nightfall and morning we drink you and drink you
> a master from Germany death comes with eyes that are blue
> with a bullet of lead he will hit in the mark he will hit you
> a man in the house your golden hair Margarete
> he hunts us down with his dogs in the sky he gives us a grave
> he plays with the serpents and dreams death comes as a master from
>   Germany
>
> your golden hair Margarete
> your ashen hair Shulamith [24]

These lines from Celan inspired Kiefer to an extended consideration of the contrast between Margarete and Shulamith, which links later to his exploration of the Exodus theme. His thinking on this theme explores the emotional context set in motion within German history. Rather than simply saying, as he might well have, that he had nothing to do with that history, which occurred before his birth, Kiefer probes and explores to uncover the vestiges of anti-Semitism within his world. In *Shulamith* he presents another version of the empty brick memorial, this time taken from Wilhelm Kreis's model of a memorial for Nazi soldiers and turned by Kiefer into a memorial for the Jews.[25] The dominant color in the picture, besides the brick, is black, which Kiefer repeatedly uses as the color symbolizing Shulamith ("your ashen hair Shulamith"). The interior of the building appears to have been scorched by flame, and the windows are blacked out by woodcut fragments, as are the flames alongside the wall, in contrast with the burning flames in Kiefer's Valhalla-like wooden room in *Germany's Spiritual Heroes* (Figure 21). He allows the staples holding the woodcuts to the surface to show, and bits of straw appear in the painting. This work is a perfect illustration of how Kiefer's thinking combines the pattern of visionary thinking with the postmodern flatbed.

We are left to determine for ourselves the significance of this theme for understanding contemporary history. Kiefer's moral commitment concerns making visible the actuality of the historical situation, rather than offering a "solution" to it. This fits in with another aspect of the "death of the subject" in postmodern art, since Jameson argues that postmodern artists and theorists have begun to give up the idea of a depth background that determines the value of signifiers. Although this may at first appear to contradict Kiefer's emphasis on going "down through the sediment," it does not really do so. Everything depends upon what we find in the sedimented layers and whether they ever yield to one clear, true depth picture. Part of what Jameson means by the loss of depth background is the loss of the idea that the signified determines the signifier. If we accept a shift to the interplay between various kinds of signifiers, which seems to be what is at issue in Kiefer's imagery, we find that "what replaces these various depth models is for the most part a conception of practices, discourses and textual play." Thus "depth is replaced by surface, or by multiple surfaces (what is often called intertextuality is in that sense no longer a matter of depth)."[26] The conflict of texts between Jewish and German experiences does not necessarily yield to any single historical or moral account.

What relationship does Jameson's concept of intertextual surfaces have to Nietzsche's conception of the psyche as a field of fluctuating intensities that only gradually organize themselves into the patterns of thought? These two lines of thought are very close together because of the fact that when we remove the idea of a prefigured depth background, we are left only with the interaction of the intensities and forms of hierarchy themselves. These often get constructed into meaningful discourses and "texts."

This same idea is implicit in Derrida's idea of "spacing," which we introduced in Chapter Three to explain the Theater of Cruelty. Derrida holds that original representation is "the archi-manifestation of force or of life":

> A closed space, that is to say a space produced from within itself and no longer organized from the vantage of an other absent site, an illocality, an alibi or an invisible utopia. The end of representation, but also original representation; the end of interpretation, but also an original interpretation that no master-speech, no project of mastery will have permeated and leveled in advance.[27]

The condition of "original interpretation" is precisely the one that thought encounters within a field of fluctuating intensities and conflicting tendencies and directions. The metaphor of intertextuality helps to reveal what is at stake in such a situation. In the case of *Shulamith* Kiefer works within the constraints of conflicting ethnic texts, their manifestation in twentieth-century history, and the poetic imagery Celan created to express their outcome.

This means that we cannot assess the work of a postmodern artist like Kiefer in terms of categories like "Neo-Expressionist" without altering our understanding of what is involved in the expression of feeling. If feelings themselves fall within an intertextual field, then they are already charged with meaning that calls, like anything else, for critical examination and reexamination. There can be no doubt that Kiefer wants us to see this point, as is exemplified by his frequent use of textual fragments and references within his visualizations. He understands the process of making a feeling visible as coincident with our ongoing effort to understand complex texts. This is confirmed by his remark, reported by Madoff, that "I can only make my feelings, thoughts, and will in the paintings. I make them as precise as I can and then after that . . . you decide what the pictures are and what I am. I go in as deep as I can in order to get farther away."[28] Since paintings *are* texts, the thoughtful consideration of what is expressed in them requires the continual return to "original interpretation." That process is never finished.

Shulamith is a perfect example of how this works, since the intensive qualities that arise from this overdetermined image generate reflection on the historical situation to which this work refers. In this respect, we see how the various types and levels of intensity created by images can give rise to substantive thought. Heidegger helps to clarify this by his analysis of affective states in Nietzsche's thought. Here is how he describes Nietzsche's view:

> A feeling is the way we find ourselves in relationship to beings, and thereby at the same time to ourselves. It is the way we find ourselves particularly attuned to beings. . . . In feeling, a state opens up, and stays open, in which we stand related to things, to ourselves, and to the people around us, always simultaneously.[29]

The attunement of ourselves to the world through feeling is similar to the way the will operates in striving "out beyond itself" in action.[30] Because the affective states cannot be confined within a merely psychological field, but occur within a symbolic-cultural field, they fall within structures of meaning lending themselves to reflection and reconsideration. Kiefer's investigation of his own feelings in such works as *Shulamith* makes us aware of this process. The barrenness of the space draws us into the context for considering the results of human hatred, and the use of the straw within the painting, like Kiefer's use of sand within *Ways: Sand of the Mark Brandenburg*, establishes our common dependence on the earth.

Although the shift toward textuality may make it appear that the role of feeling in art has been superseded, nothing could be further from the truth, as Kiefer's work abundantly demonstrates. His emotionally charged works gain their power *from* complex textual strategies, showing that the play of desire and feeling does not occur apart from texts of various kinds. Jameson especially notes that the move toward intertextuality in postmodern art does not mean "that the cultural products of the postmodern era are utterly devoid of feeling, but rather that such feelings—which it may be better and more accurate to call 'intensities'—are now free-floating and impersonal."[31] Such impersonal feelings get evoked by *Shulamith*, which in that form makes them more available for reflective thought. The shift toward a cultural basis for feelings is an essential feature of such works.

A postmodern understanding of thinking points toward such a basis for feelings and thought. Kiefer's works become sites for such expression and reflection, providing the emotional impetus for thought about forbidden topics. Yet they leave us to resolve the conflicts they present in our own way, rather than pretending to possess solutions to the problems they depict. That is one reason for the power of Kiefer's works: they confront us with the tragic nature of our own history. Although his renewal of genres (like the landscape) may seem to reinstitute organic vision and wholeness, he does so in order to draw us in like "a bee to a flower," to ponder the conflicting texts that constitute our history. Perhaps that is why he creates books, since (as Madoff reports) "a book of pictures, like a film, unfolds. There's a time factor."[32] The shift from the immediacy of consciousness toward the interpretation of texts requires such a time factor, and places us in a different relation to the past than modern thought has envisioned.

CHAPTER FIVE

Narrative Knowledge and Cultural Memory

THE ANALYSIS of the last two chapters makes it necessary that we reassess our understanding of human experience, thought, and knowledge and that we confront weaknesses in our modern attitudes toward past cultural forms. Both Nietzsche's idea of experience as a field of fluctuating intensities and Vernant's idea of tragic consciousness point toward alternatives to the modern idea of the conscious, rational subject. In tracing out the implications of these ideas, we will find it necessary to consider discarded forms of thought in a new light. Through the death of the subject we experience the loss of the dream of modernity, given such a clear expression by Hegel when he said: "To him who looks at the world rationally the world looks rationally back."[1] The circle that closed between the conscious subject and a rationally ordered world has been broken, and thinkers like Nietzsche provide a new basis for thought in the postmodern moment.

In order to come to grips with this challenge, we must examine how the loss of faith in rationally structured reality manifests itself in the visionary thinking of an artist like Kiefer, whose appeal to mythical narratives and other discarded forms of thought seems to strike a discordant note for modern viewers. We can be sure that the death of the subject cannot leave our conception of knowledge undisturbed. Kiefer's appeal to ancient myths and forms of practice that, like alchemy, were abandoned long ago by scientific thought makes this fact evident. By staging Yggdrasil and Midgard for us to ponder, he opens a space within which narratives may again be taken seriously and elemental questions about earth and cosmos may again become central for thought. The present chapter concerns these questions, which link Kiefer's form of visionary thinking to the outlooks of Nietzsche and Vernant. We will also consider Jean François Lyotard's analysis of modernity's refusal to make a place for narrative knowledge.

From the vantage point of modern rationalism, we can hardly give any credence to Kiefer's depiction of the plight of Midgard or of the threat that hovers over Yggdrasil. Lyotard gives us a clear insight into the intellectual economy that keeps such stories at bay. According to Lyotard:

> The scientist questions the validity of narrative statements and concludes that they are never subject to argumentation or proof. He classifies them as belonging to a different mentality: savage, primitive, underdeveloped, backward, alienated, composed of opinions, customs, authority, prejudice, ignorance, ideology. Narratives are fables, myths, legends, fit only for women and children. At best, attempts are made to throw some rays of light into this obscurantism, to civilize, educate, develop.[2]

By directing our attention back to this pre-scientific mentality, Kiefer's art provokes questions about the role we assign to narrative and the tendency we have to regard science as the only legitimate form of knowledge and the most reliable basis for action.

Nietzsche's conception of the Dionysian already provides part of the basis for our remodeling of the ideas of legitimate knowledge and action. The standard ideas of knowledge and action depend upon our maintaining a stable reference point for objects and a stable identity for subjects.[3] Nietzsche's concept of the Dionysian raises questions about these notions of stability, particularly if they are conceived in a static, unhistorical way. His exposure of the genealogy of consciousness contributes especially to historicizing our concepts of consciousness and action. At the same time, his genealogical analysis of values affects the modern idea of the individual and history. This is made clear especially when he says of the bourgeois individual:

> The individual, the "single man," as people and philosophers have hitherto understood him, is an error: he does not constitute a separate entity, an atom, a "link in the chain," something merely inherited from the past—he constitutes the entire *single* line "man" up to and including himself.[4]

He means that the human lineage is available to us all, providing the materials from which we may appropriate elements in the formation of our identity. Although Nietzsche's point does not alter the minimal notion of identity needed for referential discourse, it does have the virtue of opening up larger questions about cultural identity. We have seen such a process at work in Chapter Four, where we discovered the variety of sources considered by Kiefer to provide substance for his own self-examination. He seems to emphasize the multiple lineages that enter into the experience of twentieth-century humans, indicating the necessity for us to shift away from treating the individual as a separate agent who is solely responsible for ethical conduct and for the enforcement of epistemological standards. Works like *Yggdrasil* and *Shulamith* dramatize the collective roots that modern individualism tends to overlook.

Nietzsche's understanding of individual thought and action fits closely with these practices in Kiefer's art. This is evident in his earliest writings, when he considers the role of mythical thinking within tragedy. He regards Greek tragedy as an appropriation of "the old mythical garb" of earlier narratives, thereby revitalizing features of Greek religion that the emerging rational culture had put aside. He argues:

> For this is the way in which religions are wont to die out: under the stern, intelligent eyes of an orthodox dogmatism, the mythical premises of a religion are systematized as a sum total of historical events; one begins apprehensively to defend the credibility of the myths, while at the same time one opposes any continuation of their natural vitality and growth; the feeling for myth perishes, and its place is taken by the claim of religion to historical foundations. This dying myth was now seized by the new-born genius of Dionysian music; and in these hands it flourished once more with colors such as it had never yet displayed. . . . Through tragedy the myth attains its most profound content, its most expressive form.[5]

Nietzsche's idea of the revival of the mythical in the tragic arts implies the revival of a perspective that Greek rationalism had lost and that the idea of law within the polis was intended to counteract. Although Nietzsche understands that a simple return to past narrations is impossible, he nevertheless thinks that fundamental elements in earlier narrations are still functional, even if below the threshold of consciousness.

Such considerations make clear why Nietzsche regards the idea of the bourgeois individual as superficial, since it presupposes a fundamental opposition between the individual and the collective. The ideology that features individual consciousness is linked, of course, to ideas of contract and exchange, and also to the concept of the responsible agent whose actions make the economic enterprise possible. Postmodern ideas about textuality point toward a different understanding of human action, one that is able to make a place for the mythical within rational society. Deleuze and Guattari help us to understand what the textuality alternative implies:

> [There is] no reason in fact for accepting the postulate that underlies exchangist notions of society; society is not first of all a milieu for exchange where the essential would be to circulate or to cause to circulate, but rather a socius of inscription where the essential thing is to mark and to be marked. There is circulation only if inscription requires or permits it.[6]

But if marking and being marked are more fundamental than what appears before consciousness, then Nietzsche's idea that historical forces operate silently underneath the conscious projects of a people requires that we attribute a central role to collective experience. What was acknowledged in Greek tragedy, therefore, was the operative significance of ancient myths, even though they had been cast aside in favor of more "modern" Greek views. Similarly, Nietzsche holds that the impact of past inscriptions remains decisive within modern scientific culture and within modern society's ideal of democratic culture. Although the quest for valid knowledge and the dream of an improved social order were thought to depend upon the conscious mind, Nietzsche offers us reason to be suspicious of this basis and to look below the level of conscious narration. As Deleuze and Guattari see it:

> Nietzsche says: it is a matter of creating a memory for man; and man, who was constituted by means of an active faculty of forgetting (*oubli*), by means of a repression of biological memory, must create an *other* memory, one that is collective, a memory of words (*paroles*)

and no longer a memory of things, a memory of signs and no longer of effects.[7]

Nor is the active forgetting limited to the shift from "a memory for things" to "a memory of signs," since the sign-memories may themselves become subject to repression. Uncovering these repressed memories is central to Kiefer's whole work, reflecting the same task the tragic artists had in the age of Greek tragedy. Just as Nietzsche points toward the obscuring of mythological traditions in the Greek society that spawned these tragic works, Kiefer wishes to uncover the operative myths of his own society. In the case of both Nietzsche and Kiefer a genealogical analysis of values exposes the power of the inscribing socius to enter into what seem merely individual preferences and choices. Modern humans, in particular, need reminding of the operative power of this cultural deep structure, since so much of modern thought operates without sensitivity to the ongoing power of past cultural forms.

In this respect, we can see how a postmodern artist like Kiefer puts forward the collective memory by returning to a variety of myths, to the practices of the blacksmith and the alchemist, and to the historical myths of his own nation. His use of the Parsifal myth, for example, reverberates with these overtones of cultural memory. Yet such appeals to collective memory will be misrepresented if we identify them with a simple remembering of the past, diachronically conceived. Vernant helps us comprehend this when he speaks about the Greek experience of collective memory through the tragedy:

> The Muses do indeed sing . . . of the first appearance of the world, the genesis of the gods, the birth of humanity. The past thus revealed represents much more than merely the time prior to the present; it is its very source. By going back to it the process of recall seeks, not to situate events within a temporal framework, but to reach the very foundation of being, to discover what is original, the primeval reality from which the cosmos emerged and which makes it possible to understand the whole process of becoming.[8]

It is clear that Kiefer's concerns extend to such cosmic themes, since he employs several ancient thought systems to generate images about "the primeval reality" that haunts human history. In several works of the 1980s he draws materials from Jewish mysticism, from the writings of Dionysius the Areopagite on the heavenly hierarchy, and from Roman myths about Saturn, as well as from Nordic legends. A striking example is his painting entitled *Emanation* (Plate X), which like the Midgard paintings presents an elemental landscape organized around the divisions between heaven/earth and visible/invisible. The cosmic division is overcome by an emanating cloud formed from poured lead, which juts out several inches from the surface. Alongside the cloud, descending stones, only vaguely visible, fall like meteorites from the sky. These images have a complex origin, harking back equally to the alchemists' veneration of stones (which were supposed to come from heaven), to the idea in Dionysius that a "Divine Ray" makes the heavenly hierarchy visible, and to Jewish mysticism's conception of the divine substance pouring forth its attributes through the light. The latter source provides the tragic twist for Kiefer, as Mark Rosenthal interprets him:

> As the lights rain down, humanity attempts to catch them in vessels and thereby gain the benefit of these divine characteristics; evil, however, is included amidst the good. The vessels are understood to be flawed, and in the end there are more lights than the bowls can hold. The vessels shatter, loosing good and evil on earth.[9]

This cosmic dimension is a central feature of Kiefer's work, as will be made evident in Chapter Six. It brings his view into harmony with one aspect of Vernant's analysis of collective memory.

Vernant points toward the origin of actions as much as he does toward the origin of reality, since he sees the ancient Greek understanding of will and responsibility as also exhibiting traces of collective memory. We recall from Chapter Three that Vernant portrays the characters in the tragedies as caught within a circle of events that includes consequences having their source in prior events and prior generations. Thus, they cannot be held solely responsible for what happens in any particular circumstance. The relationship between the individual agent and the genealogical background is, therefore, decidedly different from the modern

conception of the self-conscious agent of action. Vernant illustrates
this with the following comment:

> The heroic legends do not present man as a responsible agent, in
> control of his actions and his personal destiny. They describe certain
> types of exploits, model trials in which ancient initiation ceremonies
> are echoed, and which use the medium of exemplary human deeds
> to illustrate the conditions necessary to acquire exceptional religious
> qualifications and social privileges.[10]

The indefiniteness of this idea of agency differs from the modern, secular idea of individual responsibility. Vernant defines it as
a "tragic sense of responsibility,"[11] according to which the flow of
natural consequences is independent of any single agent's intentions since it is impossible to control the past or to change life's
cosmic circumstances. Although a character must, like the modern agent, narrate experience as it unfolds and project actions in
terms of it, the power to control the flow of events through such
a narrative varies markedly from the modern expectation. Conse-
quently, the punishment that a character like Oedipus accepts as
the result of his actions, based on error and self-deception, seems
fitting under the conception of *tragic man,* whereas a plea for ex-
cuses would be forthcoming within the modern conception, which
places the weight of ethical responsibility on conscious intentions.
Kiefer's concern to expiate collective guilt fits right in with the
tragic conception of responsibility.

The central issue this poses for our analysis is whether this
Nietzsche-Vernant conception of tragic action, simultaneously individual and collective, can form the basis for a postmodern theory
of action. As Vernant argues with respect to Greek tragedy, it
reflects the desire of the agent of action within the city-state to
be in control of what occurs, while acknowledging the limits of
that control through the operation of forces that exceed human
powers. As Vernant sees it, this situation within tragedy depends
upon a conflict understood to be fundamental within the make-up
of humanity. "Tragic man is constituted within the space encom-
passed by this pair, *ethos* and *daimon.* If one of the two is eliminated
he vanishes."[12]

If the constitution of the agent is conceived in these terms, there is a movement between two planes of meaning for all thought and action, as we have seen through our earlier analysis of *ethos* and *daimon*. The *daimon* plane has both cosmic and genealogical aspects. This is evident in Kiefer's *Emanation* and in his collage *The Miracle of the Serpents* (Figure 18), where he creates a provocative matrix between the photographed background and four dancing snake forms, serving as metaphors for the magic rod used by Moses and Aaron during the Exodus, as in *Aaron* (Figure 12) and *The Rod* (Figure 30). Moreover, this imagery reverberates with associations of the serpent from other mythologies, such as those in shamanistic religions and in traditions dating back to the neolithic.[13] This daimonic background resonates with both good and bad consequences for humans, since to interact with the divine is to risk frustration of human purposes. In this, and many other respects, Kiefer's art is closely related to the model of tragic man.

In order to probe more fully into the questions evoked by the model of tragic man, let us consider the analysis of the postmodern condition offered by Lyotard, whose observations on the rejection of narrative in scientific thought were the starting point for the present chapter. Lyotard points out that modern civilization has a complex set of legitimation strategies, all of which relate to the idea of rational consciousness. Central to this conception is the notion of *legitimate methods* for substantiating knowledge claims, for governing ethical conduct, and for shaping political activities. If we return to Vernant here, that means that modern man features *ethos* at the expense of *daimon*. In effect, a modern person subordinates mythological and poetic narration to the causal accounts central in historical and scientific discourse. In making the case for a broader conception of knowledge and action within the postmodern moment, Lyotard argues that we must place narrative knowledge alongside scientific knowledge as another legitimate way to understand reality and human activity.

In making the case for narrative knowledge, Lyotard opposes the limitation of knowledge to scientific knowledge. In describing what is distinctive about the pragmatics of science, Lyotard points out that science adds to denotative discourse two special conditions: "the objects to which they refer must be available for repeated access, in other words, they must be accessible in explicit conditions of observation; and it must be possible to decide whether or not a given statement pertains to the language judged relevant by the experts."[14] This emphasis on repeatable observation conditions and formulation in the language of expertise differentiates scientific culture from more traditional cultures that featured narrative knowledge. He argues that narrative knowledge employs other values, including "know-how," "knowing how to live," "knowing how to listen," and similar values central to earlier cultures. Within these traditions, "knowledge, then, is a question of competence."[15] Although the standards of competence in traditional cultures differ from standards of objectivity and rational judgment in modern culture, Lyotard holds that there were operative *pragmatic* standards that governed customary forms of knowledge.

Lyotard is fully aware that this places his conception of postmodern culture in opposition to the mainstream of Enlightenment thought, which sought to displace custom in favor of purely rational standards. However, he points out that science itself, conceived as a collection of practices, had to be legitimated. How was this legitimation carried out, since it would be circular to justify science as a whole by standards that occurred in scientific thought? Lyotard argues that René Descartes provided the legitimating narrative; he could "only demonstrate the legitimacy of science through what Valéry called the story of a mind."[16] The irony is that non-narrative knowledge gained its overall legitimacy from a narrative about the origination of ideas and thoughts, thereby opening up the possibility for critical evaluation through method. By linking the legitimacy of ideas to method, Descartes sought to remove them from the genealogical context of traditional narrative justifications, thereby introducing objective control over cognitive processes.

The significance of Lyotard's argument concerning this legitimating narrative extends beyond the status of scientific knowledge, since Lyotard also argues that the same mentality entered into the interpretation of socio-political reality. Here the narrative justifying modern social practices takes this form: "the name of the hero is the people, the sign of legitimacy is the people's consensus, and their mode of creating norms is deliberation. The notion of progress is a necessary outcome of this."[17] Modern *liberal man*, in contrast with ancient *tragic man*, overthrows traditional knowledge to replace it with universal knowledge. The alleged universality depends for its credibility upon both the story of the mind and the story of the people's consensus. It is no surprise, Lyotard thinks, that the "question of the State becomes intimately entwined with that of scientific knowledge."[18] The norms that enter into both areas of modern life depend, as much as traditional forms of knowledge do, upon the plausibility of an interlinking narrative account.

Thus, what appears in modern terms to be an escape from mythological perspectives is not so different from these traditional forms of narration as we may sometimes think. Lyotard's position is, in fact, that what legitimates knowledge in either case has to do with the nature of the social bond: modern knowledge gets legitimated through operations carried out by individual, conscious minds who play a parallel role as responsible agents carrying out social performances. In other words, the social structures and knowledge structures feed back and forth on each other. Scientific knowledge helps to sustain the economic and social institutions that give rise to it and endow it with its status, and the notion of the responsible individual in bourgeois society introduces standards of rationality and evidence that help sustain scientific practices. This is one reason why the value of rational deliberation in ethical and social matters accords so well with the methodologies practiced by responsible scientific thinkers: they are a part of the same ideology.

When we contrast this modern concept of rational and liberal man with the ancient concept of tragic man, we begin to see what is at stake in this analysis. We have already seen that Oedipus could not have been responsible for his ignorance concerning his parentage, at least not in the *modern* sense of responsibility, nor could Agamemnon have been guilty (in the *modern* sense) for the curse on the house of Atreus. Yet the ancient mythological narratives hold them both responsible in the way suggested by Vernant. The *roles* they played within a tragic situation were, nevertheless, the only ones they had available. Their choices were circumscribed by conditions they did not choose, and they reflected a daimonic background that intruded into their lives in ways they could not quite foresee. What appeared on the level of conscious narration as the conditions for choice had to yield to other conditions, invisible to the participants, from the daimonic background. In rejecting the tendency of modern thought to flatten out this daimonic background in favor of an ethical description of action, Nietzsche challenges the modern conceptions of causality and responsibility. He creates a scene in *Thus Spoke Zarathustra*, entitled "The Pale Criminal," in which a criminal appearing before a judge suffers from remorse and accepts the responsibility for his deed, even though he has been sentenced to die. In so doing, he embraces the conception of responsibility under the law, which contrasts with the tragic idea of responsibility. Zarathustra points out that the pale criminal's confession of guilt helps to mask the vengeance that the judge, as representative of the people, will visit upon him in pronouncing sentence. The crucial point is that it abstracts the actions of both the judge and the criminal from the collective forces that they manifest. Nietzsche thinks that our modern idea that actions are caused by motives is wrongheaded; this is just what leads us to claim that criminals are guilty because of their intentions. Zarathustra observes:

> But the thought is one thing, the deed is another, and another yet is the image of the deed. The wheel of causality does not roll between them.
>
> An image made this pale man pale. He was equal to his deed when he did it: but he could not endure its image after it was done.[19]

By arguing that the *image* of the deed can be separated from both the deed and its motive, Nietzsche intends to raise doubts about our simplistic understanding of how actions are caused. In a related passage in *Twilight of the Idols*, Nietzsche offers a further analysis of the causality question:

> To start from the dream: on to a certain sensation, the result for example of a distant cannon-shot, a cause is subsequently foisted (often a whole little novel in which precisely the dreamer is the chief char-

acter). The sensation, meanwhile, continues to persist, as a kind of resonance: it waits, as it were, until the cause-creating drive permits it to step into the foreground—now no longer as a chance occurrence but as "meaning." The cannon-shot enters in a *causal* way, in an apparent inversion of time. That which comes later, the motivation, is experienced first, often with a hundred details which pass like lightning, the shot *follows*. . . . What has happened? The ideas *engendered* by a certain condition have been misunderstood as the cause of that condition.[20]

In this passage Nietzsche establishes the narrative context that enters into causal explanations by suggesting that the dreamer is rescued from a chance occurrence by being able to construct retrospectively a chain of events that have a meaning. There is even a hint that a whole complex of ideas fits together to make this possible: cause, irreversible diachronic time, and memory. We can now see the force of the image in the pale criminal's evaluation of his action: the meaning of what he did may be shaped retrospectively by the image, rather than by the forces that actually entered into his act.

We need not give a mystical interpretation of the daimonic to see that the idea of the tragic offers another alternative for understanding action. It exposes a multiplicity of forces that enter into any outcome, including even those we may think of as due to chance. When chance intrudes into human affairs, it means that the control we would like to exert through causality is illusory. This is precisely what enters into Camus's novel, *The Stranger*, whose chief character, Mersault, finds himself on trial for murder for having killed a man on the beach. Camus portrays the killing in circumstances that make it seem almost an accident: a matter of chance rather than a matter of intention. Yet Mersault openly acknowledges the deed, refusing retrospectively to embrace the image of the deed that everyone in the trial seeks to impose. For his refusal to show remorse, he is found guilty. This example lends support to Nietzsche's deconstruction of the background narrative entering into the modern ethos, and both Camus and Nietzsche help us to see that sketches like "The Pale Criminal" and novels like *The Stranger* should not be treated as *mere stories*.

Lyotard's analysis of the pragmatics of scientific knowledge meshes well with this Nietzschean line of thought about the genealogy of values. Similarly, Kiefer's painting confronts us with other dimensions of the daimonic than those exposed in *The Miracle of the Serpents*. We have already considered his exposure in *Shulamith* (Plate IX) of forces of power that came into being out of the German-Jewish background. In a striking watercolor version entitled *Margarete-Shulamith* Kiefer presents the image of the burning earth, which is covered by intertwining strands of gold and black, symbolizing the prototypes for the German and Jewish races. Their names mark the landscape, below the fire that threatens to destroy it. Not only does this painting identify the destructive forces of war, but it also symbolizes the other cultural forces that, though they operated for a period of time below the surface, finally erupted to destroy Germany. If we think of the role played by fire in ancient mythology, we may reasonably infer that Kiefer invokes the mythological background of Germany to practice his own ritual purification on the Margarete-Shulamith conflict. For Kiefer, it appears to be a question of an identification with the past that can only be understood genealogically, since he himself was born after the war and could not be held causally responsible for it. His need to reenact features of the past that need to be eradicated is a common element in his works, often misunderstood. Mark Rosenthal reports that Kiefer said, "I do not identify with Nero or Hitler, but I have to reenact what they did just a little bit in order to understand the madness."[21] His act of ritual purification accords well with the understanding of time found in ancient myths and with the new sense of time invoked by Derrida in describing the Theater of Cruelty, but not with the diachronic-causal sense of time.

Lyotard takes his analysis precisely down this path, arguing that a grasp of the structure of narratives in traditional cultures helps us to understand postmodern cultural developments. He argues that we must begin by assessing traditional cultures in terms of social structures that contrast with bourgeois institutions. For this purpose, he makes use of the model of language games and the relationships that govern linguistic exchanges between people. The central idea of his account is that a person's identity derives from the network of relationships that govern a culture's forms of interaction. Contrary to the bourgeois idea of the individual, Lyotard argues:

> A *self* does not amount to much, but no self is an island; each exists in a fabric of relations that is now more complex and mobile than ever before. Young or old, man or woman, rich or poor, a person is always located at "nodal points" of specific communication circuits, however tiny these may be. Or better: one is always located at a post through which various kinds of messages pass.[22]

If linguistic subjects find themselves located at posts, exchanging messages with other linguistic subjects, the pragmatic structures of these relationships become important in understanding the forms of identity achieved. Within this fluid social field, the "nodal points" represent only momentary posts, which alter as the dynamics of the exchanges shift. The more complex the relationships become—as they surely have within the contemporary world—the less there is a fixed identity for the person. This situation stands in contrast to stable forms of identity achieved within archaic and traditional societies, where the posts had a greater duration within a relatively fixed narrative structure.

A word of caution is appropriate in this context because we need to distinguish the notion of identity having to do with the makeup of the individual psyche and the bare, minimal notion of identity necessary for any cognitive discourse. The latter form of identity has to do with reference and predication and is therefore as essential to narrative discourse as it is to scientific.[23] The notion of identity tied to the individual psyche shapes itself within a shifting field of linguistic-cultural practices. This distinction is important to maintain, whereas Lyotard is sometimes careless about preserving it. Presumably discourse about ancestors within traditional cultures requires this minimum of referential identity, even if the meaning of the stories told about the ancestors keeps being altered as the myths are retold.

Returning now to Lyotard's analysis, he points toward four features of traditional narratives: (1) They involve criteria of competence, communicated through tales of the successes and failures of cultural heroes, which help to establish standards of behavior for the members of the culture. (2) They make use of a complex array of language games, without any expectation that any one of them provides the foundation for justifying all the others; although they interface with each other, they do not form a single, objective account. (3) They depend for their transmission upon the competence narrators derive from having heard the story and upon their commitment to transmitting it faithfully. (4) The time structure of narrative is unlike the modern idea of diachronic time, but is more like the time structure of music.[24] In explaining the third point, Lyotard makes it clear that the narration may be inventive without being an unfaithful transmission, since the structure of traditional myths permits a *competent* narrator to reinterpret a canonical version to one who hears the myth. The posts of narrator and hearer do not depend upon a literally correct version, but on one falling within acceptable boundaries established by a canonical version. What counts most is that the posts of narrator and hearer are affected by a third element: the myth itself.

An especially instructive example of such narrative structures is offered by James Fernandez, whose study of the Bwiti religious movement demonstrates the open, metaphorical nature of the communication between narrator and hearer. This religious movement, which occurs as a revitalization movement within African Fang culture, draws upon myths about the Fang's connections to the forest. They seek to revitalize a "primitive" culture within the modern world in order to reestablish the collective identity they had lost from colonial intrusions. Fernandez shows how the narrator-sermonizer reinterprets the traditional myths, making use of images requiring that the listeners think through fundamental puzzles about their lives and the meaning of traditional symbols. Moreover, the structure of the sermons is sufficiently open that a variety of readings is encouraged.[25]

Fernandez shows how the imagery stimulates the Bwiti to play with metonymic and metaphoric associations to make sense of the sermonizer's account. The thought patterns of the sermons center around dominant elemental images drawn from myths about the forest, the origin of life, the Fang migration from savannah to forest, and the path of birth and death. These rich images play

FIGURE 18
The Miracle of the
Serpents, 1984
Das Schlangenwunder
Acrylic and shellac on
photo bits on
photograph
58 × 83 cm
Private collection

FIGURE 19
Nürnberg, 1982
Burned wood over
oil, acrylic, and
emulsion on photo
on canvas
290 × 390 cm
Private collection

FIGURE 20
Seraphim, 1984
Oil, acrylic, emulsion, and shellac on canvas
280 × 280 cm
Private collection

FIGURE 21
Germany's Spiritual Heroes, 1973
Deutschlands Geisteshelden
Oil and charcoal on burlap
307 × 682 cm
Eli Broad Family Foundation, Santa Monica, Calif.

FIGURE 22
Yggdrasil, 1985–1986
Melted lead mounted on acrylic, emulsion, and shellac on photograph
220 × 190 cm
Private collection

FIGURE 23
Jerusalem, 1984–1986
Lead, steel skis, lead
strips, and lead
chunks over acrylic,
emulsion, shellac,
and singed spots on
canvas
380 × 560 cm
Collection of Susan and
Lewis Manilow,
Chicago

FIGURE 24
Ouroboros, 1980–1985
Shellac on photo scrap
  on photo on
  cardboard
59 × 83.5 cm
Private collection

FIGURE 25
Outpouring, 1982–1986
Ausgiessung
Oil, acrylic, emulsion, shellac, singed spots, and fern stalks on canvas; appliqué lead objects (funnel, strips).
330 × 555 cm
Louisiana Museum of Modern Art, Humlebaek, Denmark

FIGURE 26
Pittsburgh, 1984–1985
Shellac and graphite on photo on cardboard, framed
90 × 59 cm
Collection of Jan Eric von Löwenadler, New York

FIGURE 27
The Order of Angels, 1984–1985
Die Ordnung der Engel
Lead object (propeller), lead strips, lead chunks, and steel cables over acrylic, emulsion, and shellac, on canvas
330 × 550 cm
Fundació Caixa de Pensions, Barcelona

FIGURE 28
Pole, 1984–1985
Mast
Melted lead, acrylic, emulsion, and shellac on photo
70 × 105 cm
Private Collection

FIGURE 29
Pittsburgh, 1984–1985
Melted lead, acrylic,
emulsion, and shellac
on photo on
cardboard, framed
70 × 100 cm
Collection Paul Maenz,
Cologne

FIGURE 30
The Rod, 1984
Der Stab
Acrylic, emulsion,
shellac, melted lead,
and singed spots on
photo on mechanical
pulp board
70 × 100 cm
Hirshhorn Museum and
Sculpture Garden,
Washington, D.C.

FIGURE 31
The Order of Angels, 1983–1984
Die Ordnung der Engel
Lead strips over oil, emulsion, shellac, and straw on canvas
330 × 555 cm
The Art Institute, Chicago

FIGURE 32
Untitled (Seraphim), 1984
Ohne Titel (Seraphim)
Lead strips over oil, acrylic, and emulsion, on canvas
280 × 280 cm
Museum of Fine Arts, Boston

FIGURE 33
The Red Sea, 1984–1985
Das Rote Meer
Oil, emulsion, and shellac on photo and woodcut on canvas, appliqué lead strips
278.8 × 425.1 cm
The Museum of Modern Art, New York

back and forth between different levels of meaning and establish unexpected relationships. For example, Fernandez shows how water operates as one such elemental image, the forest pool being conceived as mirroring the cosmic structure of heaven and earth (above/below). Although a physical reality, the forest pool is essentially a spirit pool, associated in the Fang myths with cosmological events. Associated images, such as the raindrop clinging to the forest tree, suspended halfway between above and below, or the rainbow, which traces the path of salvation, appears in these sermons.[26] In analyzing one sermon, Fernandez observes how the water imagery helps to define the Bwiti initiates' own identity.

> [Their] origins lie in waters of various kinds. Indeed, as the sermonizer has pointed out . . . the moon has tied together the congregation in the pool. The water image continues to maintain its associative power and in further sentences brings to mind the fetus in the form of a tadpole growing, without distinction of sex, within the amniotic fluid, the bag of waters. It is to the woman particularly that the guardianship of this water of birth belongs. For it is not the man who washes his wife in the end, although in the climactic convulsions—the little deaths—of the sexual act, he provides a nurturant and protective seminal fluid for her. It is rather the woman who washes all mankind in the amniotic sac of creation.
>
> Though this, like all sermons, rests upon close observation and knowledge not only of physiological process but also of equatorial forest and fauna, one or another of these images will generally be taken as underlying and organizing. Here water is a commanding sign and exerts a principle of selection amidst the plethora of natural objects available for purposes of representation.[27]

We can see, in a similar way, that Kiefer's use of the earth as an elemental image in both the Midgard series and in paintings like *Emanation* has the effect of returning us to origins and to questions about our identity within the modern world. Like the Bwiti, he employs such symbols to evoke possibilities of revitalization and renewal in the face of destruction and rejection of past history.

The complexity of the Bwiti linguistic practices reflects a feature of Lyotard's analysis of narrative structures. He sees such structures as involving a complex of language games that are by no

means limited to denotative discourse. On the contrary, to understand the movement of the communication is to understand that
the listener must be a co-creator of the meaning to be derived. Like
the Theater of Cruelty, this opens up a form of original representation, a space within which meaning is giving birth to itself. Nor
is the meaning circumscribed by narrow boundaries, since the play
of metonym and metaphor opens up possibilities the sermonizer
may not have intended. Thus, neither the sermonizer's agency, nor
that of the listener, accords with the idea of the conscious subject,
who interprets experience in terms of a clear and evident surface.
On the contrary, by giving oneself over to the myth, one opens up
the play of difference. Part of what is at issue here, as Lyotard also
observes, is that hearers themselves may be in training to become
narrators in the future.

For our purposes, this example from the Bwiti is especially
important, since Fernandez shows how far removed such a conception of human reality is from the idea of the conscious subject, whose identity is purely individual. Contrary to this model,
Lyotard's understanding of narrative knowledge points toward an
irreducible collective element that challenges the idea of centered
and grounded individuality. Fernandez characterizes the subjects
of these transactions as "inchoate," [28] by which he means that the
forms of identity achieved are relative to the developing discourse.
Personal identity emerges more from a path than from a fixed center. This affects the way knowledge is conceived, bringing Fernandez's account close to Lyotard's understanding of narrative knowledge. Fernandez observes that " 'to know' is to have the capacity
to read signs or marks which appear spontaneously or in uncertain
circumstances. Knowing is being able to find a path by reading
available signs where no path exists." [29]

Before returning to other features of Lyotard's position, we
should note how closely Fernandez's account of Bwiti culture
dovetails with other themes of the present chapter. In particular,
the revitalization aspect of Bwiti religion reminds us of Nietzsche's idea of the dying myths of the Greek religion, which were
revitalized through tragedy. Both forms of myth were undermined, in part, by the triumph of forms of rationality that give

little credence to myths. In addition, Bwiti religion calls upon the deep structure of Fang cultural memory to help unfold an ever-changing interpretation of its symbols, even as Kiefer's works do with respect to the German cultural memory. Finally, like Vernant's conception of Greek tragedy, Fernandez's understanding of Bwiti cosmologizing points toward the operative dynamics of the daimonic in their thinking. Both traditions refer to primeval reality to help them understand the present. Yet in neither case is this cosmic background fixed and closed. On the contrary, Fernandez's account of Bwiti thinking shows how the projection of their images against the background cosmic whole requires ongoing metaphorical movement.

Returning now to Lyotard, let us consider the fourth of his points about narrative cited above: that narrative time differs from our conception of diachronic development. In comparing narrative time to music, as in the chant, Lyotard observes that "narrative form follows a rhythm; it is the synthesis of a meter beating time in regular periods and of accent modifying the length or amplitude of certain of those periods."[30] Lyotard argues that this rhythm is essential to the knowledge that is passed on:

> This kind of knowledge is quite common; nursery rhymes are of this type, and repetitive forms of contemporary music have tried to re-capture or at least approximate it. It exhibits a surprising feature: as meter takes precedence over accent in the production of sound (spoken or not), time ceases to be a support for memory to become an immemorial beating that, in the absence of a noticeable separation between periods, prevents their being numbered and consigns them to oblivion.[31]

What is conveyed through the medium of "immemorial beating" falls outside temporal causal events. Thus, a genealogical connection to the ancestors might be established through the rhythm of the narrative, putting contemporaries into the same framework as the ancestors, from whom they might otherwise feel far removed. This identification with the ancestors is a common thread in Greek tragedy, Bwiti religion, and Kiefer's art works. In all three cases, we glimpse how our values emerge from a collective background extending beyond mere contemporaries. Lyotard adds:

> Against all expectations, a collectivity that takes narrative as its key
> form of competence has no need to remember its past. It finds the
> raw material for its social bond not only in the meaning of the narra-
> tives it recounts, but also in the act of reciting them. The narratives'
> reference may seem to belong to the past, but in reality it is always
> contemporaneous with the act of recitation. . . .
>
> The important thing about the pragmatic protocol of this kind of
> narration is that it betokens a theoretical identity between each of the
> narrative's occurences.[32]

Lyotard's analysis of narrative, therefore, establishes its pragmatics
within the area we think appropriate for performances of musical and dramatic works, where what counts in the performance is
the contemporaneous value it has on the occasion of performance,
even though it also participates in "a theoretical identity between
each of [its] occurrences." For the participants in traditional culture, the act of reciting the narrative is not distanced objectively
before a judging subject, but rather it establishes a relationship to
the authority carried by the narrative itself.[33]

If we accept this line of analysis, how does that affect the overall
problem of the present chapter? We began by saying that modern
people must seemingly reject mythological interpretations in favor
of more rational accounts: those that accord with scientific and
historical ideas of causality and temporal development. However,
Lyotard's claims about the pragmatics of knowledge make it clear
that both scientific and historical analysis depend upon narrative
justifications that they cannot establish in their own terms. What
this means is that the whole enterprise of modern culture, like its
traditional antecedents, depends largely upon mythic structures for
its grounding.

This being so, can we escape the conclusion that modern
humans are in the *very same position* as our archaic ancestors? Rather
than our regarding the vision of *tragic man* as dated and outmoded,
we should treat it as a challenge to modernity's sense of superiority.
Tragic consciousness is precisely what the myth of modernity, with
its ideal of conceptual transparency, denies in every respect. Rather
than presenting a problematic vision of the world, modern humans
aspire to research procedures and forms of social investigation that

will openly reveal what we need to know to gain control. The alternative is not to give up thought, but to move in the direction of a more fragmentary and locally based form of thought. If we accept the idea that we can only move between textual surfaces, then the problematic character of our thought is fully in view.

Yet Lyotard holds that this is precisely what modern technical intelligence will not accept. The forms of legitimation central to modern society, which depend upon what he calls the "grand narrative,"[34] have lost their appeal. The grand narrative takes two forms, one of which concerns the unity of scientific knowledge (the "speculative narrative" systematically expressed by Hegel), while the other concerns social liberation (the "narrative of emancipation"). Since both forms of the grand narrative have been undermined by twentieth-century cultural developments, Lyotard believes we face a new set of conditions:

> The road is then open for an important current of postmodernity: science plays its own game; it is incapable of legitimating the other language games. The game of prescription, for example, escapes it. But above all, it is incapable of legitimating itself, as speculation assumed it could.
>
> The social subject itself seems to dissolve in this dissemination of language games. The social bond is linguistic, but it is not woven with a single thread.[35]

Because there is no single thread that unifies postmodern culture, our situation with respect to time, memory, and the past is open to redefinition. The revaluation that Nietzsche carried out is one example of what this may involve, while the Bwiti cosmologizing is another. The same is true of Kiefer's return to myths, his reconsideration of his German heritage, and his persistent exploration of cosmological questions in his recent paintings. The idea of tragic man explored in this chapter suggests that knowledge must arise from and express fragmented perspectives requiring supplementation and criticism.

Finally "the death of the subject" in postmodern art parallels the death of the narrative of the mind, which was supposed to justify science as the privileged form of knowledge. There *is* no privileged form of knowledge to be discovered by the conscious subject. Rather, both knowledge and our social life turns around a *community* of language users, narrating events and narrating about each others' behavior and seeking to create values relative to their own varieties of discourse. In this activity, postmodern art has an important role to play.

CHAPTER SIX

Cosmological and Mythical Narratives

CHAPTER FIVE HAS ESTABLISHED the need to reconsider the status of narrative, since we have shown that narrative structures stand at the foundation of even the scientific definition of reality. Lyotard's analysis of the pragmatics of mythical thinking provides insight into narrative knowledge and challenges the exclusive authority of science in interpreting what is real. Kiefer's work does so as well by the way in which his visionary thinking opens up questions about reality and history. These questions violate the assumptions of the grand narrative that has guided modern thought.

Kiefer shows us one way in which cosmological and historical myths may be appropriated to reinterpret the world view of modernity. His thinking about origins, particularly in *Emanation* and the Midgard series, reinvests ancient cosmological thinking with vitality for our age. Yet these cosmological investigations occur, as they do with the Bwiti, without any assumption that nature forms a completed whole toward which knowledge may be systematically directed. On the contrary, the openness of visionary thinking calls forth images that require ongoing exploration, like the ancient myths did in their narrative context. Similarly, Kiefer's free appropriation of historical materials indicates his understanding that sedimented historical forms require something more than an objective treatment if we are to come to grips with the actual complexity of cultural memory. In this respect, his painting practices share much in common with symbolic exchange cultures and express, like them, an intimate relationship between cosmological and historical thinking. As we have seen, this aspect of Kiefer's art embodies themes closer to the ancient tragedians than to the practices of modern liberal culture. He refurbishes thought to include daimonic dimensions just when modernity had given total authority to secular forms in shaping history.

A primary vehicle for Kiefer's synthesis of cosmos and history is his use of fire to symbolize the artist's transformative activities. "Fire on the Earth" is a theme that keeps recurring in his works. It is a theme that Kiefer associates with the practices of alchemist and blacksmith as well as with his own art. Like the ancient practitioners of the arts associated with fire, he wants his work to be a catalyst for change. Rather than allowing his art to be an instance of the productivity ideal, he wants to create "something that isn't a fabrication but a transformation."[1] Fire becomes the emblem of his emphasis upon the artist's transformative powers.

In the present chapter we will consider the connections Kiefer establishes between the earth and the transformative powers of fire. We will also consider how his restoration of mythical forms of thought fits in with cyclical conceptions of time, common in archaic cultures. This theme will bring together Derrida's idea that the Theater of Cruelty introduces an altered conception of time and Lyotard's understanding that mythical narratives are structured by a non-diachronic conception of time.

In order to begin exploring this theme, let us consider a scene from *Thus Spoke Zarathustra* in which Nietzsche's prophet describes a vision, essential to his teaching of a new outlook toward reality. Nietzsche portrays Zarathustra in conversation with a shadowy figure, identified simply as "the inquisitive dwarf":

> "Behold this gateway, dwarf!" I went on: "it has two aspects. Two paths come together here: no one has ever reached their end.
>
> "This long lane behind us: it goes on for an eternity. And that long lane ahead of us—that is another eternity.
>
> "They are in opposition to one another, these paths; they abut on one another: and it is here at this gateway that they come together. The name of the gateway is written above it: 'Moment'.
>
> "But if one were to follow them further and ever further and further: do you think, dwarf, that these paths would be in eternal opposition?"[2]

Nietzsche poses these questions concerning the "Moment" in order to challenge the Enlightenment conception of time and history. He even has the dwarf say that "time is a circle,"[3] an image that, in effect, undermines the conception of progressive temporal development. It also brings Nietzsche's concept of time into proximity with the synchronic view that occurs in mythic thinking.

What sort of present is this moment where past and future, leading to eternity in both directions, meet? The Midgard paintings provide one sort of clue, since elemental forces register themselves on the abandoned stone that lies beside the sea. Temporal development is less in evidence than the earth standing at the juncture of past and future, as the pliant medium that can register their effects. Placed against the horizon of sea and sky, the earth represents the place where humans exist and from which they look out to contemplate the cosmos. As we gaze outward, what interpretative networks define this space beyond the horizon? Nietzsche does not want us to return to the grand narrative of the unity of nature and history in such a context. Kiefer's Midgard seems to be a form of *spacing* that, like Nietzsche's image of the gate, opens up questions that modern structures of thought have put aside.

Kiefer's use of the mythological background of the Midgard and Yggdrasil narratives points in the direction Nietzsche intends. Kiefer calls forth this narrative background to interpret present reality. The image contained in the dwarf's musing that "time is a circle" implies that history is a substantial whole, which may enter into the present moment more fully than our notion of historical succession recognizes. Moreover, Nietzsche thinks that our tendency to treat the future as the focal point for the will leads us to omit possible values that are available from the past. That is why he raised the question of whether we exercise vengeance against the past by regarding it as *someone else's history,* rather than our own.

There can be no doubt that Nietzsche wishes to challenge our idea of progressive historical development, as is made clear by another of Zarathustra's questions: "And are not all things bound fast together in such a way that this moment draws after it all future things? *Therefore*—draws itself too?"[4] We must ask in what sense all things are "bound fast together," both with respect to history and with respect to the earth, for Zarathustra repeatedly teaches: "I entreat you, my brothers, *remain true to the earth,* and do not believe those who speak to you of superterrestrial hopes! They are poisoners, whether they know it or not."[5] Similarly, Kiefer's art expresses the entreaty to "remain true to the earth" in a number of ways. His staging of *Midgard* suggests as much, but even more his use of sand in *Ways: Sand of the Mark Brandenburg* (Figure 16) and of straw in many other works makes use of literal properties of earthy substance as a grounding for his vision. *Ways: Sand of the Mark Brandenburg* also brings together earth and history in a single vantage point.

These two aspects of Kiefer's staging-act converge, given the results of the previous chapter's analysis. Deleuze and Guattari give the right emphasis when they describe the earth in these terms: "The full body of the earth is not without distinguishing characteristics. Suffering and dangerous, unique, universal, it falls back on production, on the agents and connections of production. But on it, too, everything is attached and inscribed, everything is attracted, miraculated."[6] They make clear the unity of nature and culture, with the earth standing to human activity as the inscribed to the inscriber. Taking their clue from archaic cultures, Deleuze and Guattari put their emphasis upon "the cosmic egg of the full body of the earth."[7] It forms the ground on which "everything is attached and inscribed." As Deleuze and Guattari see it, primitive societies like the Dogon have such a close tie to the earth that they see it as the source from which inscriptions come, as well as that on which their own actions are registered. They also regard their own bodies as *of* the earth in the sense that any inscriptions manifested on the human body (such as body markings and body painting) establish values in a direct, physical way. This type of grounding, unlike the grounding of modern values on natural law, expresses the way filial ties shape identity, and the way alliances may form themselves from the physical relationships narrated as originating from the cosmic egg.[8]

According to this conception of the earth-human relationship, any social distinctions, such as the distinction between the sexes, and any social prohibitions, such as the one against incest, have the status of natural inscriptions, which simply reflect the way things stand within the cosmos. Thus, myths about origin from the ancestor-gods express the inexorable working of forces that are as fatalistic as is the shape and substance of the earth itself. If nature expresses itself in human form through the working of desire, then Deleuze and Guattari indicate their conviction of continuity between nature and history when they write: "There is only desire and the social and nothing else."[9] In addition they note that an elemental phenomenon like filial ties cannot be reasonably interpreted as "social rather than biological, for it is necessarily biosocial inasmuch as it is inscribed on the cosmic egg of the full body of the earth."[10] The separation of the social and the biological, which tends to be taken for granted by us, is one of those tenets of Enlightenment thought that can no longer hold conviction in postmodern thought.

It is one aspect of Deleuze and Guattari's conception that there is continuity between desire and production, since they have their base and their real effects on the earth. They insist upon the codetermination of human life by natural and social dimensions. They outline this codependency as follows:

> There is only one kind of production, the production of the real. And doubtless we can express this identity in two different ways. . . . We can say that social production, under determinate conditions, derives primarily from desiring-production: which is to say that *Homo natura* comes first. But we must also say, more accurately, that desiring-production is first and foremost social in nature, and tends to free itself only at the end: which is to say that *Homo historia* comes first. The body without organs is not an original primordial entity that later projects itself into different sorts of socius. . . . On the contrary: the body without organs is the ultimate residuum of a deterritorialized socius. The prime function incumbent upon the socius has always been to codify the flows of desire, to inscribe them, to record them, to see to it that no flow exists that is not properly dammed up, channeled, regulated.[11]

This passage states very straightforwardly the essential point about the logic of desire: desire *is* a natural function, which consists of

flows of energy that naturally invest themselves in actions, un-
less they are repressed by social measures that interfere with their
natural fulfillment. But at the same time, it also states the essential point about the logic of social organization: that the socius is
also natural, and that it shapes desire by forms of territoriality that
give human persons their identity. Neither exists without the other
within this conception of natural-historical existence.

Enough has been said to make clear the natural-social whole
within which human activities fall. We have seen also that Nietzsche's image of time as a circle implies a similarly holistic view
of our involvement with the past and future. Even as the biological and social aspects of humanity cannot be separated, Nietzsche
thinks the gate of the present draws together the divergent paths
of past and future. What this means is that the forms of identity
that shape human experience have as much to do with the past as
they do with the future. Kiefer's use of the past reflects a similar
view.

A particularly striking example of Kiefer's merger of earth
themes with historical memories is his painting entitled *Nürnberg* (Figure 19). Another example of his scorched earth series,
this painting begins as the location of the festival grounds of the
Meistersingers. The word "Festspielwiese" appears in the lower
right corner, covered over by straw that has been worked into the
painting. The charred earth, burned by Kiefer's torch, contains
references to blood and to the destruction of Nuremberg, represented by three charred pieces of wood that have been mounted on
the landscape. The historical references are staged on the scorched
earth, suggesting both the transformation of the earth itself by
human projects and its place as the ground on which a new reality
will have to be erected. The ambiguity of the status of the earth
(festival ground and surface on which humans inscribe destruction)
speaks to the double-sidedness of Dionysian reality.

The integration of the Meistersinger narrative into the inhab-
ited world indicates the degree to which Kiefer's work expresses
the unity of the earth and human history. Such an attitude is typical
of mythical narratives, and his copious use of Nordic myths is one
sign of the merging of what modernity keeps apart. A prime ex-

ample is Kiefer's use of the Wayland myth to establish an analogical link between the ancient blacksmith, whose work was shrouded in religious mystery, and the creations of the artist. According to this myth, Wayland was captured by men serving a wicked king, who had gained control over him by robbing him of a magic ring. Subsequently, Wayland's art was put to the service of the king until the queen, suspicious of the dangerous powers possessed by this worker with fire, convinced the king to imprison Wayland on an island, after severing the tendons of his legs. The song of Wayland relates the tale of how he liberated himself, taking revenge against the king by killing his three sons, burying their bodies under his bellows, and fashioning silver ornaments for the king, into which he worked their skulls. In addition, Wayland presented jewelry to the queen, composed of stones made from the eyes of her sons, and brooches to the princess made from their teeth. Finally, before escaping by wings fashioned for that purpose from lead, Wayland seduced the princess, who became pregnant with his child.[12]

In a striking painting, *Wayland's Song (with Wing)* (Plate XI), inspired by this myth, Kiefer presents another of his scorched earth settings. At the center of this landscape is a large wing, sculpted from lead, dominating the scene. This image of the triumph of Wayland, who was able to fly away from the destructive forces that had dominated his life, invokes both the powers of ancient smiths and those of the artist. The evidence from two other paintings, both dominated by the trunk of a tree, shows a wing made of lead fastened to the tree trunk in one and an artist's palette fashioned from lead in the other.[13] As in *Wayland's Song (with Wing)*, where the wing has tentacles extending between heaven and earth, apparently anchoring the wing in space, both the wing embedded in the tree and the artist's palette attach themselves to the upright tree by fingers of lead.

Why should a painter like Kiefer, who has so obviously displayed the resources of abstract painting in this work, give us images setting up an association between the artist and the ancient smith? And why does he so frequently associate the artist's role with the image of the wing?[14] The answer in both cases has to do with Kiefer's taking seriously an idea that most moderns reject:

that the renewal of our world may require that we return to ancient and archaic ideas. One aspect of this use of ancient ideas has to do with the close relationship between the earth and the sacred. *Wayland's Song (with Wing)* makes such an appeal by expressing the theme of the renewal of the scorched earth, which lies fallow awaiting the return of conditions that can make it fruitful once more—the same attitude expressed by ancient peoples toward the cycle of the seasons. His use of straw in both *Nürnberg* and *Wayland's Song (with Wing)* strikes the same note. Just as one makes use of straw to make bricks, Kiefer seems fascinated by the way earthy materials enter into the creation of real things.

The key to this line of thinking is found in Mircea Eliade (an author whose work Kiefer has read),[15] who points out that a wide range of ancient myths feature the origin of humans from the earth, particularly portraying their birth from stones.[16] On this view, stones are virtually alive, and those who extract them from the earth and transform them through fire play a role in religions from the Iron age on. Eliade writes concerning this tradition:

> Mineral substances shared in the sacredness attaching to the Earth-Mother. Very early on we are confronted with the notion that ores "grow" in the belly of the earth after the manner of embryos. Metallurgy thus takes on the character of obstetrics. Miner and metalworker intervene in the unfolding of subterranean embryology: they accelerate the rhythm of the growth of ores, they collaborate in the work of Nature and assist it to give birth more rapidly.[17]

This view of the earth, and of the sacred role of the blacksmith in relation to it, is one central motif in Kiefer's work. The tradition of alchemy is equally central, the lead wing of Wayland being only one example of Kiefer's frequent use of lead in his work to allude to the metals used by alchemists. The sacredness of the earth is alluded to, as well, by his joining of heaven and earth into one visual unit by the tentacles extending between them, as is the symbolism of *Cherubim, Seraphim*, which portrays members of the celestial hierarchy as stones.

The question of the role of wing imagery might as well be disposed of in this context, since Kiefer apparently intends to draw an analogy between the magical powers of the alchemist and the blacksmith and the magical powers that were supposed to attach to wizards, witches, yogins, and fakirs. Eliade makes the observation that metaphors of "flight" attend all these examples of people with unusual spiritual insight.[18] Moreover, in Kiefer's case this impression is supported by his frequent use of birch trees, ladders, and other symbols that merge heaven and earth together. Eliade points toward the use of these symbols within shamanistic religions, where bridge and ladder metaphors abound and where the birch tree has special significance. He notes that "the cord connecting the ceremonial birches set up for the shamanic seance is called the 'bridge' and symbolizes the shaman's ascent to the heavens."[19] The birch appears in other works, including the *Bilderstreit* book and in Kiefer's painting, *Heath of the Mark Brandenburg*.

Although his use of shamanistic symbols and his references to the alchemist and the blacksmith may appear an instance of romantic nostalgia on Kiefer's part, they go deeper than such a response would imply. They are signs of his refusal to accept a purely aesthetic function for art and of his desire to open up new interpretive possibilities within the postmodern moment. Like Nietzsche, he seems to envision the juncture of the path of the past with the path of the future as requiring that we rethink our dismissal of ancient modes of thought and reconsider our judgment of them as *merely* mythical.

Other examples point toward this conclusion. For instance, in *Seraphim* (Figure 20) Kiefer creates an image of a gigantic wing-like form, which appears to be rising toward heaven along a ladder extending upward from the earth. We must remember that the seraphs were associated with fire in the biblical account. Below it, at the base of the ladder, we find another snake, which is also a significant figure in shamanist imagery. This juxtaposition of the imagery of flight with the snake, reminiscent of Nietzsche's use of the images of eagle and serpent in *Thus Spoke Zarathustra*, corresponds to Kiefer's ambivalence toward the activities of those called "masters of fire" by Eliade. The ancient blacksmiths were both demonic and god-like, since they possessed powers that were both liberating and dangerous. Eliade observes: "Fire turned out to be the means by which man could 'execute' faster, but it could also do something other than what already existed in Nature. It was therefore the manifestation of a magico-religious power which could modify the world."[20] Because of the dangers inherent in this power, and because of the threat humans felt when interfering with matters proper to the gods, purification rituals developed in conjunction with agricultural cults, requiring blood sacrifices to placate the gods and guarantee an abundant harvest. In other societies the expiation of the gods took on different forms, but often included some element of suffering or sacrifice. What is common to these different manifestations, however, is the ambivalent response they reveal toward the powers possessed by the masters of fire. Kiefer reflects this ambivalence, treating fire in many different paintings as possessing both positive and negative aspects. Besides the "scorched earth paintings," he introduces the fire theme into his spacious empty halls. In one example, *Germany's Spiritual Heroes* (Figure 21), we find torches symbolizing various figures from German history lining the walls. We have also observed the association of fire with the artist in *Painting of the Scorched Earth* (Figure 17) and in *Nero Paints* (Figure 8). Kiefer presents the palette form in both these cases in association with the charred landscape.

His use of past religious symbols and ideas, which we tend to regard as outmoded forms of mythological thinking, becomes the means by which Kiefer challenges us to reconsider our project of the prediction and control of nature within a technological age. Essential to this aspect of his work is the frequent use he makes of symbols of alchemy. Our attitude toward the alchemists tends to be that they were pre-scientific experimenters whose ideology so dominated them that it kept them from developing a truly rational, scientific view of nature. There are, however, features of the alchemical tradition that have other implications that Kiefer wishes to draw to our attention. One of these has to do with the idea of creation, which plays such a role in the ideology of modern art. Eliade argues that the alchemical tradition has continuity with the older blacksmith tradition. He argues that the ideology of the masters of fire included a different conception of creation from the one dominant in Judeo-Christian civilization:

The conception of a *"creatio ex nihilo"*, accomplished by a supreme heavenly deity, has been overshadowed and superseded by the idea of creation by hierogamy and blood sacrifice; we pass from the idea of *creation* to that of *procreation*. This is one of the reasons why, in the mythology of metallurgy, we come up against the motifs of ritual union and blood sacrifice.[21]

We have already seen how Kiefer uses the bowl of blood in *Parsifal II* to remind us of blood sacrifice, even as Stravinsky does in *The Rite of Spring*. The power of the Dionysian includes the excesses of behavior that have been celebrated in such rituals, which we regard as barbaric. At the same time, the idea of procreation has its positive side, which Deleuze and Guattari have brought forward in their analysis of the close relationship between desire and the direct achievement of value.

The question of how to overcome the negative implications of the ideologies that governed the masters of fire is not so simple as it might at first appear. Kiefer, after all, is the painter of the tragedy of German civilization, who repeatedly confronts his compatriots with reminders of the outcome of their own "civilized" values. The distance between blood sacrifice and the scorched earth is great, although the degree of destruction has taken a quantum leap in the more "civilized" approach to the transformation of the earth. Our uses of fire, no longer under the hold of primitive beliefs, have consequences that might well stimulate us to reassess critically what we believe, rather than acting as if our ancestors' beliefs reflected a merely primitive or child-like mentality.

Apart from these considerations, a conception of procreation instead of creation *ex nihilo* has another significance for our understanding of the artist's activity. It is obvious that Nietzsche's genealogical approach to values fits closely with this idea of procreation, and we have already seen how the appropriation of images and narratives from the past fit, in Kiefer's case, with a less psychologically based idea of creation. Within the symbolic rituals of the masters of fire, meaning is born in a way that contrasts with the projection of meaning by the modern artist.

The question of the role of fire appears in other forms in Kiefer's painting, especially in the works of the 1980s that make

use of lead to provoke a dynamic opposition between ancient ideologies and the contemporary world view. For example, in another
version of *Yggdrasil* (Figure 22) Kiefer presents the image of a tree
ignited by a fire from the sky. What is this imagery about? We
remember that Yggdrasil is the name for the gigantic ash tree in
Nordic mythology, the *axis mundi,* which is "vastly tall, its top en-
veloped in the clouds, while from it comes the dew that falls in the
valleys. It stands there evergreen, beside the spring of life (Urd-
quelle). At the top of the tree is an eagle (Adler), in its branches are
four stags (Hirsche)." [22] The four stags appear in a lyrical watercolor treatment that shows them frolicking along the forest edge,
where they seem in close harmony with their environment. However, according to the myth, Yggdrasil is under constant threat
from the stags, "who eat the buds on its branches," from a dragon
who lives at its base and "gnaws away at its roots," and from an
"incredible number of worms, snakes, or serpents," who "also in-
fest its subsidiary roots." [23] Thus, the forces of nature are not, in
this case, supportive of the life and destiny of the World Ash. But
Kiefer associates these destructive forces, in Figure 22, with the
masters of fire, since the cloud into which Yggdrasil reaches is
blackened and a scorched lead blob reaches down from the sky. In
his similar painting from the "Breaking of Vessels" series (1986),
the molten lead is even more obtrusive, covering over part of the
tree, with lead funnels having been attached to the base, appearing
almost like sap funnels attached to tap the juices from the tree.

This complex imagery has important reverberations in Kiefer's
larger work, since if we regard the tree of life as a symbol of hope,
as Kiefer himself would have us do, we must also recognize that he
repeatedly portrays it as under threat, not only from the dragons,
snakes and stags that undermine its life-supports, but also from
humanity itself. Why does Kiefer associate the alchemist with this
destructive potential, since in other respects he appears to champion the masters of fire as precursors of the creative spirit Kiefer
wishes to promote? This question immediately begins to take on
another aspect when we look at Kiefer's rendering of *Yggdrasil* in
Plate V, one of Kiefer's "cardboard" collages, reflecting the same
techniques he had employed in the Exodus series. In this version,

we see the photographic image of a tree in front of an industrial pylon, to the left of which we see a factory. Molten lead has been poured over this background, after the top half had been over-painted in black. The obvious allusion is to the relationship be-tween the alchemist's project of transforming nature by fire and the modern industrial transformation of the materials of the earth and its attendant ecological threat. This disturbing analogy ap-pears to be intended to confront us with the fact that, even when the intentions of humans are honorable, as they surely were with the alchemists, who sought only to understand what was most essential about the world, nevertheless the activities by which they transform nature have consequences that are sometimes severe. This consideration moves us toward the heart of the matter with respect to Kiefer's allusions to alchemy, since what began as an ideology of reverence for nature, and ritual identification with the powers by which it could be transformed, has the surprising up-shot, if Eliade is right, that "on the plane of cultural history . . . the alchemists, in their desire to supersede Time, anticipated what is in fact the essence of the ideology of the modern world."[24] What Eliade means is that the alchemical tradition's transformative im-pulses became changed, over time, into the project of *control* over nature by scientific reason. What began in reverence and insecurity, requiring rituals of purification and expiation, has now become the subject of experiment and control within a stridently secular context. Kiefer, it seems, wishes to expose this conflict within his Theater of Cruelty.

In associating the creative process with the positive potentials of alchemy, Kiefer reiterates an attitude toward alchemy shared by Artaud, who spoke of the Theater of Cruelty as an "alchemi-cal theater."[25] Artaud's understanding of the connection between the Theater of Cruelty and alchemy is that both address, "on the spiritual and imaginary level," the transformation of "matter into gold."[26] Kiefer has adopted a self-image as alchemist-artist, push-ing the manipulation of molten lead to new heights in his works of the 1980s. One colossal painting, *Jerusalem* (Figure 23), has been covered over completely by lead, which was later peeled back to expose abstract painted forms underneath. Like the historical Jerusalem, Kiefer's painting seems to register the suffering entailed in its history of creation and destruction.[27] The transformation into gold even appears, with gold leaf being embedded into the sky above, and two steel skis placed in the center of the painting indicate the upward and downward cycle that Kiefer derived from Jewish emanation theory. Again Kiefer introduces the cosmic dimension into his alchemical works.

The purpose may be expressed well by Artaud:

> Now these conflicts which the Cosmos in turmoil offers us in a philosophically distorted and impure manner, alchemy offers us in all their rigorous intellectuality, since it permits us to attain once more to the sublime, *but with drama,* after a meticulous and unremitting pulverization of every insufficiently fine, insufficiently matured form.[28]

The process of alchemical transformation, therefore, can be a model for art in two respects important to Theater of Cruelty thinking: it reflects a rigorous process of experimentation and alteration, which undermines the everyday understanding of reality, and it is unremitting in subjecting the materials under investigation to "pulverization," until something not otherwise evident may be made evident. This is what the metaphor of transformation into gold is supposed to convey.

In one of his painted books, *The Painter's Studio,* Kiefer gives evidence of such thinking, presenting one page on which a glowing fire appears, down among the blackened rocks, the apparent source of a molten lava that flows over the page. The refining fire of the alchemist is therefore like the glow of the artist's fire, both of them having the potential to expose gold, although through processes that take on different forms in the two cases. In speaking about this aspect of alchemy, Eliade points out that the color symbolism in alchemy, which centers around four colors (black, white, yellow, and red), has to do with the stages by which matter gets transformed. In the *nigredo* (black) phase, the alchemist symbolizes both death and the color that substances assume when they reach their molten, chaotic state when broken down by fire.[29] Kiefer's own use of black harks back to this tradition, and one of his black landscapes even bears the title *Nigredo*. At the same time, the role of lead in Kiefer's work of the 1980s gets clarified if we attend to what Bettina Knapp says about alchemical processes: "*Nigredo*, the blackening process, was comparable to chaos, the *massa confusa* that existed before the separation of the elements; it is a state in which matter is reduced to an almost liquid condition or has become a 'quality of the *prima materia*.' Lead corresponds to this stage."[30] Kiefer's extensive use of molten lead in the Exodus series to symbolize the pillar of fire and the pillar of cloud that guided the Israelites on their journey from Egypt appears and reappears in works like those in the Yggdrasil series and in *Emanation*. It is evident that his use of the symbols and colors of alchemy directs us toward something corresponding to the spiritual journey involved in the separation into the elements. In the Yggdrasil works, the black sky and the molten lead appear even to be attacking the Tree of Life.

Yet as we have seen in *Varus* and in *Cherubim, Seraphim*, Kiefer counterbalances this theme of destruction with white, which symbolizes resurrection and renewal for the alchemist.[31] For Kiefer, too, white often symbolizes renewal, overcoming the charred ruins left by the blackened remnants of fire. Yet that phase can only come, in alchemical thinking, after the phase of the *nigredo,* in which what already exists must be broken down. The significance of this for our concerns can be seen by considering another of Kiefer's recent collages, *Ouroboros* (Figure 24), which is a collage cut-out of a serpent, overlaid on a photographic background of the night sky. The title refers to a Gnostic symbol of a serpent who eats his own tail, symbolizing a condition of ignorance that corresponds to the undifferentiated state of matter in its molten state. It may also refer, psychologically, to a condition of childhood before the child has been separated from the parent.[32] Metaphorically, it may refer to the condition of contemporary humanity before the cosmos, as we engage in the beginning of the space age. Before entering into the phase of the alchemical white, we may first have to undergo our contemporary *nigredo*. Ouroboros might turn out to be, in the space age, Mithgarthsorm (cp. p. 40) in another guise.

Kiefer's continued use of imagery from ancient times effectively requires that we examine the guiding assumptions of modern thought, including those of modern art. By painting huge landscapes, which evoke dark feelings, he reminds us of some of the practitioners of the abstract sublime, although he has moved outside their practices by reintroducing figurative and historical references. Several other works of the 1970s and 1980s have the scope and reach of the works of those painters, yet in paintings like *Outpouring* (Figure 25) Kiefer captures our ambivalent feelings about the modern world by presenting a painted black cloud, hovering between heaven and earth, its shape alternately suggesting the black smoke of some subterranean fire or scorched elements emanating from the sky. This latter suggestion reminds us of the clouds of lead in other works, like the one reaching down in *Emanation*. The upward/downward movement is reinforced by dried fern stalks arranged along the whole face of the painting in the vertical axis. Alongside the cloud, Kiefer has fastened another of his lead funnels. In another gigantic painting, *The Coast*, Kiefer portrays a vast barren land mass, stretching below a narrow band of the sea, punctuated throughout by sculptured funnels fastened to the surface. The most prominent of these, a large inverted one, appears over a space low in the painting, from which a reddish glow is faintly visible, making it possible for us to see it as a hood or chimney, mounted over a fire. The other funnels have been mounted on pedestals, fashioned from lead-covered stones or metal slabs. The whole dark, black-brown ground displays faint patches of bright color showing through the thick impasto, and the sculpted forms jut out like artifacts turned up in some archaeological dig. This painting summarizes in its many aspects the line of development we have been pursuing with respect to the masters of fire and the close connection their activity had to the earth. This line of reasoning reinforces the starting point of the chapter, where nature and history intertwine within mythical thinking.

The view we have been developing establishes a close relationship between desire and the earth, which is both a receptacle responding to human works and a source from which materials may be drawn and transformed. But we have also seen how it was a source of mystery for the early masters of fire. In the space age, that mystery may have been transferred to the stars, where Ouroboros symbolizes the lack of understanding that greets our contemplation of the cosmos, when we are honest with ourselves. Kiefer's version of alchemical theater sets us to wondering about how well we are equipped to enter the age of cosmic adventure. Are we really confident that the coded systems on which we rely are adequate guides for the challenges of this new age? That is the sort of question we contemplate in the light of Kiefer's works.

We need to ask, finally, about the broader significance of Kiefer's uses of the past, which invoke Nordic myths, the ancient blacksmith, the alchemist, ancient Jewish scriptures, and the historical tradition of the Germans in a provocative mix. Is this just an eclectic mix, which grasps whatever is at hand as the subject for art works, or does it signify something more important about developments in postmodern culture? The answer is obvious from our analysis, since Kiefer's perceptive mind offers an interpretation of past and future that binds them into a single cycle. The attitude this expresses also fits into the Dionysian view of existence, according to which both desire and social reality arise from the earth and continue to reflect it as source. Such a view implies a respect for mythological modes of thought missing in more abstract modes of modern thought. In taking myths more seriously than this modern view does, Kiefer challenges the way these abstractions dominate our thinking, thereby opening up new possibilities for us to consider.

Once again, Eliade helps us to get our bearings in adjusting to this aspect of Kiefer's practices, since his analysis of the relationship between myth and reality gives just the emphasis we need to put these developments in proper perspective. Eliade points out that, in those societies where myth is still living, it supplies models for human behavior that "establish and justify all human conduct and activity."[33] Although the justification strategies of archaic peoples have little appeal for us, since we cannot believe what they believed, Eliade points out that, nevertheless, they provide views of reality, rather than mere false stories. Not only do they provide narrations of the origin of the world, but also "myth narrates a sacred history."[34] He explains:

> Myths . . . narrate not only the origin of the World, of animals, of plants, and of man, but also all the primordial events in consequence of which man became what he is today—mortal, sexed, organized in a society, obliged to work in order to live, and working in accordance with certain rules. If the World *exists,* if man *exists,* it is because Supernatural Beings exercised creative powers in the "beginning". But after the cosmogony and the creation of man other events occurred, and man *as he is today* is the direct result of those mythical events, *he is constituted by those events.*[35]

Eliade is speaking of how humanity gained its sense of mortality through those events, but the mythic view of history, which treats humans as "constituted by those events" recounted in the myths, stands also in opposition to ideas of linear historical development in modern thought. Kiefer makes a serious use of the past because he believes, with Nietzsche, that that past helps to constitute what we are.

In Nietzsche's case, these considerations led him to create a genealogical analysis of history to challenge the usual linear, causal account. What this means is that our moral values, for example, may be constituted by ancestral events long forgotten, the remembering of which casts new light on those values. They cannot, of course, be simply remembered, but a deconstructive analysis may expose their origin in practices that alter their significance. For example, Nietzsche argues that the concept of moral guilt had its origin in debtor-creditor relationships, stemming from the ancient exercise of power before "civilized" society was founded.[36] This means that moral conscience is a phenomenon founded on a different basis than a direct grounding in consciousness. In fact, Nietzsche holds that genealogical analysis provides an explanation for the founding of consciousness, since he believes that occurred from a need for the creation of memory. He asks: "*For what purpose,* then, any consciousness at all when it is in the main *superfluous?*" His answer is that "*consciousness has developed only under the pressure of the need for communication;* that from the start it was needed and useful only between human beings (particularly between those who commanded and those who obeyed); and that it also developed only in proportion to the degree of this utility."[37] This implies that if we wish to understand ourselves, we must uncover the sources of our convictions and outlook through genealogical analysis, rather than taking the deliverances of consciousness at face value. As in psychoanalysis, Nietzsche's account points out how mythological elements may enter into the formation of our values without our consciously recognizing the role they play.

Enough has been said to give us a way of understanding Kiefer's uses of myths and historical occurrences that distinguishes them from a merely eclectic or nostalgic use. If we think of myths in the proper way, they may be regarded as ways of remembering the human past. Eliade points out that this is precisely their function within archaic societies, since they provide a narrative about the past that helps to explain the present situation of a people. From this point of view, it is important to grasp the structures of the whole cycle of time, contrary to the modern view of history. Eliade argues:

> A "primitive" could say: I am what I am today because a series of events occurred before I existed. But he would at once have to add: events that took place *in mythical times* and therefore make up a *sacred history.* . . . In addition, while a modern man, though regarding himself as the result of the course of Universal History, does not feel obliged to know the whole of it, the man of the archaic societies is not only obliged to remember mythical history but also to *re-enact* a large part of it periodically. It is here that we find the greatest difference between the man of the archaic societies and modern man: the irreversibility of events, which is the characteristic trait of History for the latter, is not a fact to the former.[38]

This passage puts the critical issue in a nutshell with regard to Kiefer's uses of the past. His works invoke a mythological perspective, which asks that we consider history in a different light from the one that has dominated modern thought and that still dominates within our present technological concerns. It may be that our life within the collective, like the forms of tribal life that shaped humanity in the past, may make it appropriate that we reconsider a view of the earth and cultural memory that has been subordinated to the dream of a rational world. In Part III we will consider how Kiefer's artistic approach points in that direction.

PART

III

Humanity in the
Postmodern Moment

We have seen in Part II that both Kiefer's appropriation of past cultural forms and his cosmic visions undermine received views of nature, human nature, historical development, and art. We have utilized ideas from Nietzsche, Lyotard, Vernant, Deleuze and Guattari, Eliade, and Jameson to clarify Kiefer's challenge to the world view of modernity. In his appeal to mythical narratives, Kiefer makes human identity dependent on texts and traditions rather than on the conscious subject; and he treats the earth as our local cosmic base instead of projecting human life against nature as an ordered whole. These shifts reflect his fundamental challenge to forms of modern thought.

Kiefer's conception of the artist represents a similar change. Instead of conceiving art as emanating from the creative subject, Kiefer appropriates historical materials wherever he finds them, transforming them from their original condition to pose questions and conflicts for our age. Contrary to the ideology of the individual subject, these works tap collective sources and are addressed to collective meanings. We have seen how he turns away from a linear idea of history toward an open relationship to a variety of past sources. This leads Kiefer into open conflict even with his teacher, Joseph Beuys, with whom he disagrees about the artist's relationship to history. The following exchange occurred in a 1986 roundtable discussion:

> *Beuys:* . . . No god can help us anymore; we have to become gods ourselves.
>
> *Kiefer:* That's a completely linear way of looking at things, with a beginning and a goal.
>
> *Beuys:* There's always a beginning and an end.
>
> *Kiefer:* But I always see more circular movements and the simultaneity of everything. [1]

Thus, Kiefer's view of history places him outside the artistic vanguard, who want to be the visionaries who usher in future history. In Beuys's case, that means moving toward the era when every person would be an artist. Beuys articulates the dream in this way: "I see modern art as an important phase in which the signals are erected for a coming culture which no longer depends upon a collective culture but rather emanates from a free individual, who creates his own culture." [2] Part II has shown the limitations of this form of individualism and exposed Kiefer's resistance to it in his uses of the past.

That is why Kiefer's program is far more than an extension of the modernist program, since he raises doubts about modernist ideals and erects a more ambiguous outlook in its place. Among other things that means the loss of the vanguard artist's sense of clear historical direction. That is one reason Marxist critics have been suspicious of regressive tendencies in Kiefer's works. In Part III we will consider these issues about the artist, history, and the future. In particular the question of technology will help us to focus on the most salient features of the debate, since technologists share with Marxists and the artistic avant-garde the dream of progress. Kiefer's rejection of this future orientation becomes clear through a series of collages and paintings in which he juxtaposes images of technological structures with those referring to the masters of fire. His purpose is to stage the conflict between modern humanity's desire to dominate nature and ancient people's close kinship with the earth. This will be the theme of Chapter Seven.

We can begin to see what is at stake if we remember Baudrillard's charge (quoted in Chapter Two) that even Marxism reflects an "anthropological consensus with the options of Western rationalism in its definitive form acquired in eighteenth century bourgeois thought. Science, technique, progress, history—in these ideas we have an entire civilization that comprehends itself as producing its own development."[3] The loss of this consensus calls forth two different responses. The first is skepticism, represented by Baudrillard's own conclusion that the productivity ideal continues to shape our activity, even though we have lost faith in the ideology of progress. The upshot, as he sees it, is production according to codes and simulation systems that have no purpose beyond what they produce. In contrast, Kiefer's response is to revitalize symbolic cultural forms that were supposed to have become outmoded in modern epistemological paradigms. The contrasting responses of Baudrillard and Kiefer to this situation are representative of two major strands in postmodern culture. This will form the topic for Chapter Eight.

Modern culture's ideal of universal truth is one barrier to twentieth-century people's finding insight and guidance in earlier forms of myth. Even modern artists have succumbed to that ideal, turning to abstraction in part because of their desire to establish a universal and international art. Now that the modern "anthropological consensus" has lost its credibility, Kiefer holds that today the "artist is forced to wander around and settle down somewhere temporarily. That is the opposite of Internationalism, because Internationalism is coming from one place; it sees everything from one location.

One thinks internationally." [4] *By restoring the local and temporary to center stage, Kiefer expresses one of the strongest currents of postmodern culture.*

Yet, as we will see in Part III, an emphasis on temporary and local perspectives takes several different forms. In Kiefer's version local traditions occur against the backdrop of cosmic reality and mythical time, thereby retaining much of the mystery that governed symbolic-exchange cultures. Unlike Baudrillard's skepticism about reality in the age of the simulacrum, Kiefer insists upon the similarity between postmodern humanity and ancient humanity. He seems to say that the loss of historical direction corrects the arrogance of modern people. He says to Beuys, who is suspicious of Kiefer's rejection of avant-garde ideals:

> My attitude can be a form of resignation. But not a resignation that one has when you can't go on, but rather a resignation in relationship to breadth, i.e. in view of the not-yet-known possibilities. And with resignation I am not thinking about giving up. But I am not also trying like Münchhausen to pull myself out of the swamp by my own hair; rather I am trying to see where I find myself in eternity, and I intend to present that which surrounds me. [5]

It is this attitude that distinguishes Kiefer's outlook both from the avant-garde program and the postmodern advocates of the simulacra.

CHAPTER SEVEN

Technology and Historical Progress in the Postmodern Moment

L YOTARD'S DESIRE to reinstitute narrative knowledge (discussed in Chapter Five) raises a fundamental challenge to modern thought and the ideals formulated during the Enlightenment. Since he denies that science is the sole model for knowledge and that scientific rationality is the paradigm for all legitimate judgment, Lyotard poses a direct challenge to the received tradition of modernity, including its ideas about technological improvement and the reshaping of our history. Lyotard's rejection of the grand narrative leaves us wondering what the new guides will be in the postmodern moment. Central to Lyotard's position is the following paradox:

> A postmodern artist or writer is in the position of a philosopher: the text he writes, the work he produces are not in principle governed by preestablished rules, and they cannot be judged according to a determining judgment, by applying familiar categories to the text or to the work. Those rules and categories are what the work of art itself is looking for. The artist and the writer, then, are working without rules in order to formulate the rules of what *will have been done*.[1]

Kiefer endorses just such an assessment of the situation of the contemporary artist. As the result of historical developments in the twentieth century (particularly the two world wars), he holds that "the structures are broken. The class that establishes structures is missing. And what makes our profession so difficult today is that we have to be both: we must set up the laws and, at the same time, oppose them."[2] If familiar rules and categories cannot be applied to judge what is created or written, then what basis have we for defining reality and projecting future actions? This problem,

which constitutes the main topic of the present chapter, is central
to our evaluation of postmodern culture.

Some Marxist critics have characterized postmodern art and
philosophy as misguided and regressive because of their rejection
of the modern ideals of rationality and social consensus. For example, Jürgen Habermas has been critical of them for betraying
the ideals of Enlightenment thought, since he believes those ideals
provide the best chance for us to marshall energy for social change.
In describing what he calls "the project of modernity," Habermas
speaks of the efforts of Enlightenment thinkers "to develop objective science, universal morality and law, and autonomous art
according to their inner logic."

> At the same time, this project intended to release the cognitive poten-
> tials of each of these domains from their esoteric forms. The Enlight-
> enment philosophers wanted to utilize this accumulation of special-
> ized culture for the enrichment of everyday life—that is to say, for
> the rational organization of everyday social life.[3]

Habermas hopes to revitalize these ideals to help create a society
fulfilling the ideal of "communicative rationality."[4] When Habermas asks whether we should "try to hold on to the *intentions* of the
Enlightenment, feeble as they may be, or . . . declare the entire
project of modernity a lost cause,"[5] he defines the watershed that
separates him from postmodern developments. His desire to renew
the modern humanistic program separates him from postmodern
thinkers, leading him to characterize both Foucault and Derrida
as "young conservatives." (No doubt Lyotard and Kiefer would
receive the same epithet.) Habermas objects to their endorsement
of "a decentered subjectivity, emancipated from the imperatives
of work and usefulness." He continues: "They remove into the
sphere of the far-away and the archaic the spontaneous powers of
imagination, self-experience and emotion."[6] As we have seen in
Part II, both the redefinition of human agency and an altered attitude toward the archaic are central characteristics of postmodern
thought.

Two forms of revitalization confront one another in this clash
between Habermas and the advocates of the postmodern. While

Habermas wishes to revitalize Enlightenment ideals, which treat the mythical and the archaic as irrational historical remnants, the advocates of the postmodern desire another form of revitalization by which past perspectives become integral to contemporary life. Rather than endorsing the modern idea of progress in history, these postmodern thinkers emphasize the common core of human interest shared between our predecessors and contemporaries. When Lyotard argues that the grand legitimating narratives of modernity have lost their credibility, he is expressing the postmodern loss of faith in the *intentions* of the Enlightenment, especially those relating to the superiority of the modern over all other cultural forms. If we are to follow Lyotard in this diagnosis, we must ask what legitimation strategies are to take the place of those to be discarded, especially since, unlike the members of traditional cultures, we lack a single communal narrative to supply other forms of legitimation. Although Habermas shares many of the critical concerns about bourgeois culture that motivate Lyotard's rejection of the grand narrative, he wants to know to what we may appeal in their place.

A major flaw in modern thought, cited by both Foucault and Lyotard, is its failure to recognize the close link between knowledge and power. The whole culture has been grounded on the priority of knowledge over other concerns, the assumption being that moral and social values will improve as we gain additional understanding. Yet if Lyotard is right in claiming that the autonomous judgment of the mind is the necessary basis for both forms of grand narrative, and if we can no longer endorse that story, then it would appear that both the unity of knowledge and the social emancipation it was supposed to foster can no longer be defended. Lyotard argues that the idea of autonomous reason is particularly suspect today, since the development of logic in this century has shown that no axiomatic system can be justified on purely logical grounds. What this means is that science itself depends upon pragmatic considerations, since even the rules of formal systems "cannot themselves be demonstrated but are the object of a consensus among experts. These rules, or at least some of them, are requests. The request is a modality of prescription."[7] Therefore, science depends upon a community of experts whose consensus is necessary to sustain its authority. Lyotard's point is that, whatever we may think of the value of scientific thought, neither it nor any other form of rationality can provide a neutral, unbiased basis for improving society and history. He holds that science, like any other social structure, is entangled in questions of power. That is one major reason why the grand narrative of the unity of knowledge is dubious. Lyotard concludes: "Obviously, a major shift in the notion of reason accompanies this new arrangement. The principle of a universal metalanguage is replaced by the principle of a plurality of formal and axiomatic systems capable of arguing the truth of denotative statements."[8] If no form of reasoning is universally authoritative and if all forms depend upon consensus among the relevant experts, then we must accept a more pluralistic culture than the one envisioned during the Enlightenment. Lyotard summarizes his stance with the imperative: "Let us wage a war on totality; let us be witnesses to the unpresentable; let us activate the differences and save the honor of the name."[9] Rather than the grand narrative, Lyotard holds that we must learn to be content with "the little narrative"[10] and to recognize the pragmatic background entering into every form of knowledge claim.

One outcome of the rationalist program of modern thought, and its attendant idea of historical progress, has been the full development of technology. Perhaps no other area of modernity has been taken more for granted, since the intention to improve the human condition seems to require all the technical ingenuity at our disposal. Nevertheless, the results have not always been desirable. An artist like Kiefer has much to show us about the tension between these intentions and their consequences. In a number of related works, he displays the conflicts engendered by the triumph of technology. For example, his collage entitled *Pittsburgh* (Figure 26) confronts us with the skyline of an industrial wasteland, whose power lines, upright supports, and factories define an upper space, rising over a rift below. The abstract form of the lower section could symbolize a strip mine, which has yielded up its fuel for industrial production, or alternatively a mound of industrial debris dumped along the river valleys of that beleaguered city. Staged in

Kiefer's Theater of Cruelty, these images generate disturbing questions we repress when we uncritically place ourselves within the technological project. The murky wash covering the surface, like the film that appears on the windows of all our Pittsburghs, raises doubts about what is seen and what is hidden. The downward flow of the yellow pool of liquid at the top, contradicting the upward thrust of the power posts, reminds us of the sun's rays that would bathe this space, cutting through the grey atmosphere if it were one of nature's foggy mornings. Yet what we confront here is not nature but human artifacts thrown up to challenge nature.

Like so many of Kiefer's works, this one seems bent on fulfilling Artaud's dream of turning the theater into a "*site of passage* for those immense analogical disturbances in which ideas are arrested in flight . . . in their transmutation into the abstract."[11] The disturbances finding their site in this work concern conflicts between the cultural goals of the technological age and the setting that reflects its effects, as well as conflicts between Kiefer's way of doing art and what is prescribed within the terms of modernity's understanding of the place of art. *Pittsburgh*, beginning in photographic realism, presents a twilight scene, partially obscured from view by collage pieces pasted over the bottom half and by the painted liquid emanating from the sky above. Kiefer undermines our sense of realism by his deliberate violation of its photographic terms, thereby setting up reverberations between his own activity and the depicted space of industrial reality. While we may think of nature as the common base for both industrial and artistic creations, Kiefer establishes a conflict between our desire to be at home within nature and our desire for more Pittsburghs. The effect he achieves through these analogical disturbances is to deconstruct the source of our desires, exposing the conflict between nature-desires and our desire for the triumph of technology and its productive processes. We have already discussed another collage, *Johannisnacht* (Plate IV), where this same opposition is evident.

Kiefer poses questions about values taken for granted in the modern world. His imagery confronts us with the reality of the industrial world and its association with the productive processes in art itself. Lyotard extends these questions further by highlighting additional difficulties arising from contemporary computerized and electronic forms of technology. They make the relationship of technology to power even more threatening. What we see in *Pittsburgh* is only one consequence of a culture Lyotard describes as dominated by "the principle of optimal performance." This means that technology is "a game pertaining not to the true, the just, or the beautiful, etc., but to efficiency." [12] The hidden order of values implicit in this performance principle, although masked under the ideal of rational progress, concerns the operation of wealth. Lyotard adds:

> What happened at the end of the eighteenth century, with the first industrial revolution, is that the reciprocal of this equation was discovered: no technology without wealth, but no wealth without technology. A technical apparatus requires an investment; but since it optimizes the efficiency of the task to which it is applied, it also optimizes the surplus-value derived from this improved performance. [13]

Even scientific research is implicated in this interface between technology and wealth, since research requires technological instruments. The intertwining of the value of knowledge with capitalism's performance principle is one reason Lyotard expresses suspicion about the rationalist values of Enlightenment culture.

Although Habermas and other Marxists would readily assent to many features of this diagnosis, the loss of the narrative of social emancipation appears too serious for them to embrace Lyotard's whole approach. Frederic Jameson wants to keep the rhetoric of emancipation alive. Here is his description of the interface between technology and capitalism:

> I want to avoid the implication that technology is in any way the "ultimately determining instance" either of our present-day social life or of our cultural production: such a thesis is of course ultimately at one with the post-Marxist notion of a "postindustrialist" society. Rather, I want to suggest that our faulty representations of some immense communicational and computer network are themselves but a distorted figuration of something even deeper, namely the whole world system of present-day multinational capitalism. The technology of contemporary society is therefore mesmerizing and fascinating, not so much in its own right, but because it seems to offer some privi-

leged representational shorthand for grasping a network of power and control even more difficult for our minds and imaginations to grasp —namely the whole new decentred global network of . . . capital itself.[14]

Although Jameson thinks the emphasis must be placed upon the power structure of international capitalism, the emphasis in Lyotard and in Kiefer's work applies more to the world view that sustains that economic system. In neither case is it technology per se that serves as an explanatory principle.

In considering further Habermas's desire to revitalize the grand narrative of social emancipation, we must ask whether it is possible to separate the desire for social improvement from the rest of modernity's world view. In order to pursue this question, we need to return to Kiefer's depiction of the conflict between our desire for technology and our desire to be in harmony with nature. Although this theme links Kiefer's outlook to Romanticism, the force of his imagery drives home considerations beyond a merely Romantic outlook. A collage like *Johannisnacht* implicitly pushes us toward these larger questions, which ask about our *relationship* to nature within the technological project.

Heidegger has argued that "we shall never experience our relationship to the essence of technology so long as we merely conceive and push forward the technological, put up with it, or evade it."[15] Neither the enthusiastic promotion, nor the toleration, nor the evasion of technology, meets the challenge of understanding its transformative power, which extends even to changing humanity itself. Heidegger sees fundamental alteration in everything:

> The earth and its atmosphere become raw material. Man becomes human material, which is disposed of with a view to proposed goals. The unconditioned establishment of the unconditional self-assertion by which the world is purposefully made over according to . . . man's command is a process that emerges from the hidden nature of technology.[16]

Part of what is hidden within the technological project is a mentality that, even in its artistic manifestation, celebrates the self-assertive act of creation and production, refusing to acknowledge

nature as a limit of any kind. This attitude is one primary differ-
entiation between modern humanity and the more archaic views
symbolized by the concept *tragic man.*

The meaning of what nature *is* has undergone change even
from what it was in early modern thought, when nature provided
the normative base for human activity. We remember here Baudrillard's claim that this outlook "is shattered in the 18th century
with the rise and 'discovery' of Nature as a potentiality of *powers,*"
resulting in "Nature's entry into the era of its technical domination."[17] We remember, also, Baudrillard's charge that Marxist
thought never quite confronts its own endorsement of the productivity ideal within this altered view of nature.

One of the issues between Habermas and thinkers like Lyotard,
therefore, has to do with the status of nature in our world view.
One reason for Lyotard's defense of mythological traditions, as
well as Kiefer's use of them in his works, is the challenge they offer
to a conception of nature under human dominance. One appeal
of the idea of *tragic man* is its recognition that nature sets limits to
human desire. Here is how Heidegger sees the ancient alternative:

> To be beheld by what is, to be included and maintained within its
> openness and in that way to be borne along by it, to be driven about
> by its oppositions and marked by its discord—that is the essence of
> man in the great age of the Greeks. Therefore, in order to fulfill his
> essence, Greek man must gather [*legein*] and save [*sōzein*], catch up
> and preserve, what opens itself in its openness, and he must remain
> exposed [*alētheuein*] to all its sundering confusions. Greek man *is* as
> the one who apprehends [*der Vernehmer*] that which is, and this is why
> in the age of the Greeks the world cannot become picture.[18]

What Heidegger means is that the modern idea of representation
turns the world into a picture and humans into beings able to alter
what is thereby pictured, whereas ancient people found themselves
caught in cross currents requiring their response to forces they
could scarcely comprehend.

The conflict between the modern world picture and such ancient perspectives is the subject of *The Order of Angels* (Figure 27),
shown in Kiefer's "Breaking of Vessels" exhibition. It is another

work on the theme of "Dionysius the Areopagite." This large canvas is dominated by a huge sculpted propeller blade, mounted diagonally across the center of the canvas. A number of lead-covered stones, dangling from the canvas on strands of metal, are labeled with the names of the celestial hierarchy. Inscribed in the upper left corner, we find "Dionysius Aeropagita [sic]— die Ordnung der Engel" (Dionysius the Areopagite—the Order of Angels). Some of the stones are mounted from the top of the canvas, while others appear to be hanging from the propeller blade itself. This strange, brooding painting conveys dissonant energy that attracts and repels us simultaneously. What is particularly striking about it in the present context is its juxtaposition of the sculptured propeller blade with the stones representing the heavenly hierachy; both the stones and the lead covering them have been crafted by the artist. This allusion to alchemy on Kiefer's part within the context of the propeller blade reminds us of Eliade's association of the masters of fire with modern technology (discussed in Chapter Six). At the same time, Kiefer sets up reverberations between his own artistic creation and the crafting activities involved in these other domains.

However, more is at stake than a simple association of technology, alchemy, and artistic productivity. The dissonance created by this canvas evokes a hidden conflict of values between modernity and more archaic views of nature. Perhaps that conflict is never far from the surface, even though we seldom note it. Baudrillard adds additional dimensions to these considerations when he argues that modern science "presents itself as a project progressing toward an objective determined in advance by Nature. Science and Technology present themselves as revealing what is inscribed in Nature: not only its secrets but their deep purpose." [19] Yet what is inscribed there reflects the human purposes involved in technology and capitalist production. The result, says Baudrillard, is: "Everything that invokes Nature invokes the domination of Nature." [20] This attitude produces a separation between humans and nature uncharacteristic of archaic cultures. The alternative Baudrillard sketches (discussed briefly in Chapter Two) is a view of nature in primitive cultures where humans are intimately involved with natural forces and the mode of life is shaped by symbolic exchange. He adds that "in his symbolic exchanges primitive man *does not gauge himself in relation to Nature*. He is not aware of Necessity, a Law that takes effect only with the objectification of Nature." [21] Baudrillard holds that even Greek rationalism never produces the kind of outlook toward nature found in modern science, because the Greeks did not separate humans from nature either.[22]

The dissonance evoked by Kiefer's use of the propeller blade and the lead-covered stones cuts, therefore, to the heart of the modern world view and exposes alternatives present in antecedent cultural forms. His revitalization of mythical forms of thought, like Lyotard's advocacy of narrative knowledge, is a fundamental challenge to modernity's view of nature. We have already considered other examples from Kiefer's *oeuvre* that make a similar statement, such as the Midgard and Yggdrasil paintings, but the connection to the technological project is made more explicit in the present work.

Baudrillard's depiction of cultures built around symbolic exchange adds other considerations important for the present chapter. Just as he argues that the meaning of nature has been rewritten "according to the code of production," he holds also that the idea of history has been shaped in the same way.[23] While nature provides the spatial locus for production, history provides the temporal framework. Baudrillard holds that those cultures based on symbolic exchange have experienced the world in a radically different way. He criticizes Marxist anthropologists who have tried to impose concepts about production and surplus value onto such cultures. He notes:

> Primitive "society" does not exist as an instance apart from symbolic exchange; and this exchange never results from an "excess" of production. It is the opposite: to the extent that these terms apply here, "subsistence" and "economic exchange" are the *residue* of symbolic exchange, a *remainder*. Symbolic circulation is primordial. Things of functional use are *taken from* that sphere. . . . Nothing remains because survival is not a principle. *We* have made it one. For the primitives, eating, drinking, and living are first of all acts that are exchanged: if they are not exchanged, they do not occur.[24]

That is why their view of both nature and human experience has to be distinguished from the one present in the modern technological project. It is unlike either the bourgeois ideology about humanity and nature or the Marxist alternative to it. Baudrillard adds:

> Nothing is ever taken from nature without being returned to it. Primitive man does not chop one tree or trace one furrow without "appeasing the spirits" with a counter-gift or sacrifice. This taking and returning, giving and receiving, is essential. It is always an actualization of symbolic exchange through gods. The final product is never aimed for. There is neither behavior aiming to produce useful values for the group through technical means, nor behavior aiming at the same end by magical means. . . . Magic in the sense that we understand it, as a direct objective appropriation of natural forces, is a concept only negatively determined by our rational concept of labor. To articulate magic and labor in one "interior and indivisible unity" only seals their disjunction. It ultimately disqualifies primitive symbolic practices as irrational in opposition to rational labor.[25]

The reciprocity involved in this outlook between humans and nature and between community members contrasts with modernity's understanding of reality. Kiefer's work helps us to see this.

These considerations make it clear, as well, why we cannot treat science and technology as neutral in their outlooks. Heidegger warns us of self-deception when we try to do so. He describes the technological project as an *enframing* project by which reality gets arrayed for human consideration in a specific way: reality is that which reveals itself within the framework of research activity.[26] Kiefer appears in two of his collages to have reversed this enframing act, exposing it by hanging it on the wall for us to see. In *Pole* (Figure 28) the photographed image of a power pole, overpainted in black, suggests a metaphoric exchange between this conveyer of electrical power and the superstructure of a ship. Or in another version of *Pittsburgh* (Figure 29), the upward reach of a tree, an industrial pylon, and several supports for power lines are set in counterpoint to the downward flow of molten lead, which seems to ooze from the sky above (reminding us again of the Yggdrasil series). Both the solidified crust of the lead and the scorched surface, reflecting the effect of its heat, break the visual dominance of the pylon, partially obscuring it from our view. By joining these allusions to alchemy with the images of technological and industrial production, Kiefer creates a paradox for us to consider.

It is a paradox, rather than a simple parallel, because of the gap in world view we have just considered. Kiefer repeatedly displays that gap for us to ponder. We remember his large landscape, *Outpouring* (Figure 25), discussed above. The gap is made even more evident in Kiefer's collages from the Exodus, which use lead overlays to symbolize the pillars of cloud and fire that guided the ancient Israelites from Egypt. In *The Rod* (Figure 30) we see the rod of Moses and Aaron superimposed on a photograph of a modern power post. Like the cloud above with which it makes contact, the rod is fashioned from lead. Except for the emanating lead, nothing of the hidden god is evident, making us doubt whether the Israelites were following Jahweh's signs or some imagined dream of their own, like the alchemist's dream of gold. This translation of *powers* into imagistic form gets at the paradox Kiefer wants us to ponder.

Although the Exodus theme may appear far removed from Kiefer's Pittsburgh skyline, his fertile intelligence sets up reverberations between it and the modern technological setting. The uncertain source of the pillar of cloud in the Exodus series raises the same question as our modern following of the siren song of technology by which we strive to realize our dreams. We remember, also, Kiefer's gigantic painting, *The Coast*, which, like Kiefer's earlier scorched-earth paintings, shows us images of destructive actions and forces, reflecting one outcome of our historical efforts to build a world to our own liking. Kiefer seems to be saying that in creating we destroy, requiring that we assess the one against the other in our judgment of what we have accomplished.

The destructive potential of our technological designs arises from the confident self-assertiveness that Heidegger warned about. Our project entails that "the world is purposefully made over according to . . . man's command," but without the limits to human power that were acknowledged in earlier forms of culture. Heidegger argues that, although modern research methods have contributed greatly to human life, "the revealing that holds sway throughout modern technology does not unfold into a bringing-forth in the sense of *poiesis*":

> The revealing that rules in modern technology is a challenging [*Herausfordern*], which puts to nature the unreasonable demand that it supply energy that can be extracted and stored as such. But does this not hold true for the old windmill as well? No. Its sails do indeed turn in the wind; they are left entirely to the wind's blowing. But the windmill does not unlock energy from the air currents in order to store it.
>
> In contrast, a tract of land is challenged into the putting out of coal and ore. The earth now reveals itself as a coal mining district, the soil as a mineral deposit.[27]

In contrast, the ancient metallurgists treated the earth and its materials in a completely different manner.

In this context it is useful to remember Lyotard's association of mythical narrative with the rhythms of music, because it helps to deepen our grasp of the pre-moderns' involvement with nature. It will be remembered that Lyotard held that the rhythmic development of archaic ritual is to be distinguished from what modern thought finds essential to musical rhythm: orderly measure. In a similar vein, Deleuze and Guattari associate rhythm with what they call "smooth space," which they contrast with "striated space," or space organized according to the grid. The land lends itself to striated subdivisions, while the air and the sea are two examples of smooth spaces. The waves of the sea provide a concrete emblem of rhythm understood as fluid regularity. Kiefer's Midgard images seem to visualize a form of smooth space. Deleuze and Guattari add:

> There is indeed such a thing as measured, cadensed rhythm, relating to the coursing of a river between its banks or to the form of a striated space; but there is also a rhythm without measure, which relates to the upswell of a flow, in other words to the manner in which a fluid occupies a smooth space.[28]

Whereas modern thought favors a conception of striated space, and utilizes it to create measured subdivisions within nature, the response to nature through symbolic exchange seems more in keeping with rhythm understood as the "upswell of a flow." Deleuze and Guattari point out how the ancient arts of metallurgy entail this relationship to earthly materials, rather than treating them merely as mineral deposits. This dynamic conception of the earth gains further elaboration through their comparison of metallurgy to music:

> If metallurgy has an essential relation with music, it is not only by virtue of the sounds of the forge, but of the tendency within both arts to bring into its own, beyond separate forms, a continuous development of form, and beyond variable matters, a continuous variation of matter: a widened chromaticism sustains both music and metallurgy; the musical smith was the first "transformer." In short, what metal and metallurgy bring to light is a life inherent to matter, a vital state of matter as such, a material vitalism that doubtless exists everywhere but is ordinarily hidden or covered, rendered unrecognizable, dissociated by the hylomorphic model. Metallurgy is the consciousness or thought of the matter-flow, and metal the correlate of this consciousness.[29]

The essential fluidity of materials calls forth the rhythms of the smith's hammering. Similarly, Kiefer's painting often seems a response to such flows within smooth space.

The smooth space portrayed in the Midgard paintings, expressing the mysterious, unfathomable openness of nature we experience when we stand before an expanse of the sea, both threatens us and gives rise to a promise of renewal. Just as the celestial stones of *Cherubim, Seraphim* (Plate VII) promise the renewal of fallow, burned earth furrows, so the poetic reach of the Midgard paintings, challenging our understanding of the earth's reality, inspires new possibilities for conceiving of the world. The deconstructive power of these images exposes our penchant for treating the earth and its materials as a mere "standing-reserve"[30] awaiting our use of them and suggests, in contrast, that our hope rests with the revival of ancient attitudes toward the earth.

There are two respects in which Kiefer especially relates to these considerations about metallurgy and the ancient arts. The first of these concerns a relationship to the earth and to materials, which he perceives as radically altered by the Industrial age. He asks why it is that our age produces things of such poor quality.

> How do we have this lowering of standards now, all these ugly things? Industrial fabrication and new materials have led to unlimited possibilities of forms. There is no natural limitation, i.e. no necessary structure any more, like the materials of wood and stone would demand. That is a symbol for the situation. One has to decide now. Why are ugly things being produced which no one needs? Because one doesn't have a framework for a decision yet. One manufactures simply everything which is technically possible.[31]

This is as clear a statement of the culture of the simulacra as one could get, and it is clear that Kiefer sees materials of the earth like wood and stone as calling forth a different response. This explains, in part, the association of the stones in *Cherubim, Seraphim* with the heavenly hierarchy.

The second respect in which Kiefer relates to the outlook described by Deleuze and Guattari concerns the artist's role as a *transformer*. This concept applies not only to the transformation of materials, but also to the way artists are related to their work. Deleuze and Guattari suggest that the smith becomes a transformer through sensitive attunement to the material. Like Prometheus, who brings the fire of the gods to earth, the artist becomes the medium through which reality is revealed. When Beuys questions Kiefer about the nature of artistic work, Kiefer's reply makes it clear that his view is close to the one Deleuze and Guattari describe. He says: "Artistic work is to perceive as precisely as possible that which goes through me as an example for that which goes through others. I can only do that which goes through me. But that doesn't mean that it's valid only for me." [32] It is this *relationship* to reality that Kiefer consistently alludes to in associating the artist with the scorched earth. The artist as transformer—this concept stands in clear opposition to the notion of creation through individual will.

Although we may never again subscribe to the beliefs contained in ancient mythologies, they are nevertheless useful in making us aware of forgotten forces that shape our responses to the world. If we are to comprehend Midgard, thrust up as a lonely stone within the cosmos, we must risk raising doubts about the closure we thought we had gained when we believed we could, at last, master nature. Heidegger notes an important role for art that seems to fit Kiefer's practice in the work we have been considering:

> Because the essence of technology is nothing technological, essential reflection upon technology and decisive confrontation with it must happen in a realm that is, on the one hand, akin to the essence of technology and, on the other, fundamentally different from it.
> Such a realm is art. But certainly only if reflection on art, for its part, does not shut its eyes to the constellation of truth after which we are *questioning*.[33]

Just as Nietzsche portrayed Greek tragedy as revitalizing the lost mythical traditions of earlier Greek culture, we see Kiefer's art as revitalizing our own tradition through such questioning.

Lyotard's emphasis on narrative knowledge establishes a context within which to assess this aspect of Kiefer's art. As we have seen, his defense of narrative knowledge is not intended to undermine science as a form of knowledge but only to challenge its exclusive claims. Moreover, he wants us to see that scientific discourse involves language games that, like any other language games, are relative to the assumptions guiding the practice. He is particularly anxious that we understand that the justification strategies in science lack foundational justification rules and should, like any other human enterprise, be judged pragmatically.

We cannot, of course, simply oppose traditional narratives to scientific discourse since we cannot reconstitute the authority structures they once had. Because of this, any appeal we make to ancient perspectives can only have a critical function in relation to our own assumptions. One result of that critical outlook is to challenge modern thought's dependence on the universal. That is why Lyotard introduces the notion of the little narrative as a counterweight to the grand narrative of the unity of all knowledge. He wants us to face up to the necessity of embracing fragmentary and differential perspectives. Such an approach reminds us of Kiefer's observation, quoted earlier, that the contemporary artist "is forced to wander around and set himself down somewhere temporarily."

That was in the context of Kiefer's own rejection of the modern artist's quest for universality. Lyotard's desire to "wage war on totality" implies the rejection of any form of interpretation or action that would project itself on the whole of reality. In this respect, we wonder whether Habermas is not the conservative.

This postmodern vantage point recognizes the actuality of science, technology, and late capitalism without embracing every aspect of the world view that made them possible. Lyotard argues that the idea of positive science must yield to a new form of discourse where counterexamples, paralogies, and the active use of imagination become typical aspects of scientific practice. Although Lyotard offers little to clarify exactly what this would mean, he clearly wants to associate his outlook with the idea that science's own development has undermined commitment to an exclusive form of scientific rationality. In this vein he says:

> Returning to the description of scientific pragmatics, it is now dissension that must be emphasized. Consensus is a horizon that is never reached. Research that takes place under the aegis of a paradigm tends to stabilize; it is like the exploitation of a technological, economic, or artistic "idea." It cannot be discounted. But what is striking is that someone always comes along to disturb the order of "reason."[34]

It is one thing to relocate science within social practices and quite another to endorse every aspect of what Lyotard has to say about scientific pragmatics. Although he is right to challenge the notion of consensus expected under the Enlightenment ideal of science, his own formulation is misleading in overstating the case for dissension and plurality. Postmodern philosophy must still include minimum features of rationality, even while challenging the forms of universality that were claimed in modern thought. Even the little narratives will have to be framed in terms of a consensus sufficient to keep the language games functional. This requires, as Joseph Margolis has argued, that we distinguish "with care the logical requirements of unicity or individuation from the prejudice of certain substantive (premodernist or modernist) presumptions of unity or fixity of nature."[35]

Nor does the model of the little narrative mean the absence of rules in every form. As we saw in the beginning of the chapter, Lyotard believes that the task is "to formulate the rules of what *will have been done,*" rather than appealing to the rational ideals lost when the conception of nature supporting them was transformed. In the postmodern conception, Lyotard notes, science "is not without rules (there are classes of catastrophes), but it is always locally determined." [36] Similarly, our ethical and social outlook must become locally determined. But *how* local they may be is problematic. As Kiefer's works show, local appeals open into much larger perspectives.

Even as the idea of "smooth space" implies an indefinite horizon and the presence of forces we cannot entirely control, so the idea of local determination affirms that our perspectives are fragmentary and will require supplementation. Although Lyotard's reference to the "little narrative" may appear to underrate broad empirical generalizations, there is no reason, in principle, why his view must imply anything of the kind. Likewise, social change on a broad scale may be possible without any totalizing claims.

An artist like Kiefer helps us to visualize what a locally determined form of culture might entail. His appeal to Nordic myths, to the Exodus, to practices of ancient metallurgy, and to the traditions of ancient religions helps to expose possibilities for renewal that Enlightenment ideals foreclosed. It also reasserts the importance of the *daimonic* against the opposition to any such dimension of experience in a technological world. In discussing the values inherent in technological culture, Kiefer asserts that "everything which was special and is related to the cosmic is thrown out. Workmanship is no longer at stake but jobs." [37] By questioning modern humanity's dependence on a world of fixed rational structures, Kiefer hopes to stimulate our return to the cosmic and to a conception of history as a "smooth space" from which we can freely draw. These are the sources from which we may supplement our limited understanding of reality. By appealing to this larger perspective, Kiefer hopes to gain the distance from which to view the limitations of a culture based on mere simulacra.

CHAPTER EIGHT

The Postmodern Habitat

T HIS STUDY of postmodern culture has focused on several fundamental challenges to the world view of modernity, including critical questions about the received views of nature, human nature, historical development, and the role of art itself. The fascination archaic cultures have held for postmodern artists like Kiefer presents the modern outlook with one of its greatest challenges. Their refusal to cast aside these voices from the past, and indeed their dissemination of certain ancient values and ideas, has raised serious questions about the modern understanding of the human habitat. One clear example is the cosmological vision of Kiefer's Midgard paintings, which reinvest the natural world with mystery and an atmosphere of uncertainty that is alien to the modern objectifying strategy.

In order to pursue this theme, let us return to Baudrillard's analysis of symbolic exchange in archaic cultures. Their outlook poses an alternative both to the modern conception of nature and to the idea of the autonomous individual. Under the model of symbolic exchange, human powers emerge within the natural habitat and remain bound by its limits, whereas modern humanity wants to exert active control over its environment. Unlike the modern worker, an artisan (such as a blacksmith) "is not in the situation of an autonomous individual, in a position of 'control,' that is, of productive exteriority."[1] The external relationship between modern workers and their materials is fundamental to our ideas of production and creation. Although modern artists may remind us in certain ways of the receptivity and metaphoric thinking found among ancient artisans, they still strive to become autonomous creators. It is important to remember how Baudrillard differentiates archaic attitudes from the modern emphasis on autonomy: "Symbolic reciprocity is very different from this. *The symbolic must never be confused with the psychological.* The symbolic sets up a relation of exchange in which the respective positions cannot be autonomized."[2] Although he uses the term "symbolic exchange" to describe transactions within archaic cultures, he also notes that the kind of exchange is unlike modern transactions between two contracting individuals. Rather, "there is an order of exchange and an order of fate."[3] When seen in light of this distinction, all modern transactions operate outside the order of fate. From this point of view, the Marxist distinction between use value and exchange value does not begin to approach the idea of symbolic exchange. Both use value and exchange value reflect the modern psychological orientation, which creates a gap between human purposes and nature. In contrast, the reciprocity ideal in archaic cultures means that humans must respond to natural conditions, since fated conditions are simply there calling for a response.

The logical outcome for modernity, as Baudrillard sees it, is the creation of a culture so far removed from nature, and so much under the performance principle, that we now encounter "the hyperrealism of simulation,"[4] by which he means that our habitat has begun to shift from nature to a simulated substitute. Created environments, like Disneyland, become the emblems of contemporary culture. Insofar as the capitalist performance principle expresses the preoccupation we moderns have with creating our own world, then nature as an original disappears, and created simulacra become the new reality. Modern art, too, gets caught within this network of new products. In contrast, a postmodern artist like Kiefer wants to revive a close relationship to the natural habitat and thereby challenge the historical project of modernity. The contrast between hyperreality and the natural habitat is the central topic of the present chapter. We must consider whether the simulacrum idea has advanced so far that any attempt to recover another view of the habitat would simply be anachronistic.

Not only did the members of archaic cultures enjoy an intimate relationship with nature, but we have seen that they also had close association with their ancestors. Their cyclical understanding of time made it possible for them to think of having contemporaneous relationships with earlier generations. In contrast, our modern idea of time and history confines individual experience to the present and individual action to the bearing it has on the future. The past can play a causal role, but only through intervening conditions. In addition, the past may provide information to guide present conduct. This becomes particularly significant in contemporary culture, where what is stored up in computers can be drawn upon to shape the future. Symbolic reciprocity is nowhere in evidence, since the past in its modern guise is, like nature, simply there to be exploited.

Frederic Jameson argues that, as the productivity ideal has gained in significance, the "past is thereby itself modified: what was once . . . the organic genealogy of the bourgeois collective project" has now "itself become a vast collection of images, a multitudinous photographic simulacrum."[5] He means that it has become like a vast picture album, no longer the organic basis for collective memory and projected meaning, but now only a set of remnants that are responded to in terms of contemporary desires. This elevation of the image over the source creates, as Baudrillard sees it, a culture where "simulators try to make the real, all the real, coincide with their simulation models."[6] In this connection, it is useful to remember Baudrillard's description quoted in Chapter Two:

> The real is produced from miniaturised units, from matrices, memory banks and command models—and with these it can be reproduced an indefinite number of times. It no longer has to be rational, since it is no longer measured against some ideal or negative instance. It is nothing more than operational. In fact, since it is no longer enveloped by an imaginary, it is no longer real at all. It is a hyperreal, the product of an irradiating synthesis of combinatory models in a hyperspace without atmosphere.[7]

Baudrillard himself suggests that this new habitat, resulting from humanity's own ongoing creation, can produce "joy in an excess of meaning" or "joy in the microscopic simulation which transforms the real into the hyperreal."[8] It can produce "effects of giddiness" that are "induced by the connections,"[9] but the connections are without direction or purpose. The question this poses for us is whether the *hypermodern* will be the determining definition of humans in the postmodern moment.

If we were to read it only in these terms, rather than in the terms we have been pursuing through Kiefer's works, the resulting understanding of the past would be that it would become, as Jameson claims, a collection of stereotypical images. The new realism this requires would make us "aware of a new and original historical situation in which we are condemned to seek History by way of our own pop images and simulacra of that history, which itself remains forever out of reach."[10] When we remember the stereotypical images in Kiefer's Ways of Worldly Wisdom series, we see that, in one respect at least, his use of past images agrees with Jameson's diagnosis. Nevertheless, we have shown that Kiefer has other purposes that separate his work from the game of images played within such art forms as pop art and photorealism.

Jameson argues that such artistic practices reflect a growing belief that reality has no *depth,* making the postmodern moment "the moment of a radical eclipse of Nature itself":

> Heidegger's "field path" is after all irredeemably and irrevocably destroyed by late capital, by the green revolution, by neocolonialism and the megalopolis, which runs its superhighways over the older fields and vacant lots, and turns Heidegger's "house of being" into condominiums, if not the most miserable unheated rat-infested tenement buildings. The *other* of our society is in that sense no longer Nature at all, as it was in precapitalist societies, but something else.[11]

This striking passage states, in an essential way, the problem faced by advocates of the postmodern. The power of the diagnosis may make it appear that we must endorse this loss of depth and learn to take joy in creating varieties of simulacra. However, Jameson does not himself intend that we draw this conclusion. Like Baudrillard, Jameson wants us to perceive the outcome of the productivity values of modern capitalism and to recognize it as the cultural dominant of our time; but unlike Baudrillard, Jameson recognizes the need for us to develop "cognitive maps" that will help us comprehend this situation. Because he believes that the old cognitive maps now fail us—such as the ones that look to nature for guidance —Jameson foresees a pedagogical role for art in helping us to create new cognitive maps.[12] As he sees it, this is the major challenge for art in the current cultural context.

One of the reasons Kiefer's work is so important for our time is that he advances this pedagogical function for art. Yet there seems to be an uneasy tension between what he wishes to teach and what Jameson envisions in this situation. The cosmic space of his Midgard paintings, for example, seems to return to nature, in some sense, rather than to accept Jameson's idea of the "radical eclipse of nature" and the loss of depth. Later in the chapter we will be more prepared to evaluate this apparent difference between Jameson and Kiefer. For the present, we can say that the Midgard paintings present a setting that *appears* to conflict with the hyperspace both Baudrillard and Jameson find characteristic in the contemporary world.

Jameson argues that a number of architectural works have come to symbolize the creation of the hyperreal, including the Bonaventura Hotel in Los Angeles: "I believe that, with a certain number of other characteristic postmodern buildings, such as the *Beaubourg* in Paris, or the Eaton Centre in Toronto, the *Bonaventura* aspires to being a total space, a complete world, a kind of miniature city."[13] The desire to create and live within such hyperspaces contrasts markedly with the desires expressed within ancient cultures, and seemingly with the space represented in Kiefer's paintings.

What are the crucial differences between these two types of space, which seem to make Kiefer's sensibility out of character with the creators of hyperreality? For one thing, Kiefer's work does not aspire to a total space but conveys instead a cosmic space that is fragmentary and ambiguous. His return to nature is not a return to the view that arose after the Renaissance, but rather to the *earth,* conceived as a primeval and elemental space set within the cosmos. This setting is evident in *The Order of Angels*, 1983–1984 (Figure 31), which does not represent a scene from nature so much as it does a theatrical setting for elemental forces. Unlike the striated visual space we associate with nature in the modern period, the setting depicted here is a smooth space, providing a vague location that requires that we, like the Israelites on the desert, wander and find our way toward a promised destination. The only problem for us is that the destination is not clear. The tragic coloration of the landscape only adds to our sense of uncertainty and potential danger.

Kiefer's tragic vision again undermines our confidence in the modern world view. He strategically places the snake amidst the stones, which are linked by strands of metal to the names of the celestial hierarchy on the horizon line. Kiefer repeatedly locates us on the axis between sky and earth, indicating the elemental habitat of our existence. The snake, a sign of both threat and renewal, appears and reappears in these cosmologizing scenes. In Kiefer's 1984 untitled work on the Seraphim theme (Figure 32) it appears at the base of a ladder rising between heaven and earth. We remember that both the ladder and the snake are shamanistic symbols, and in this context indicate hope and aspiration within the blackened space of Kiefer's cosmic theater. This reading gets reinforced by the lead strips. Seraphs, too, are a sign of refining and renewal, since they represent the flaming and kindling powers of fire.

From the vantage point of modern humans, who wish to extend their dreams of domination by creating total spaces like the Bonaventura, the smooth space of Kiefer's cosmic landscapes can be disconcerting. The fluidity of this space suggests his denial of any kind of fixed essence, making Kiefer's visualizations instances of something Deleuze and Guattari describe as nomadic thought:

> The classical image of thought, and the striating of mental space it effects, aspires to universality. It in effect operates with two "universals," the Whole as the final ground of being or all-encompassing horizon, and the Subject as the principle that converts being into being-for-us. . . . It is now easy for us to characterize the nomad thought that rejects this image, and proceeds otherwise. It does not ally itself with a universal thinking subject, but on the contrary with a singular race; and it does not ground itself in an all-encompassing totality, but is on the contrary deployed in a horizonless milieu that is a smooth space, steppe, desert or sea.[14]

Kiefer's visual spaces appear to go on indefinitely, like the horizon alongside the sea, seemingly fitting within no completed whole.

They convey the sense of an indefinite background, extending without any discrete boundaries. In contrast, Jameson points out that the designers of the Bonaventura do not even want it to be a part of the city, but rather want to create a self-contained space, totally set apart.[15] It may, nevertheless, serve as a cognitive map of the city space by giving a miniaturized version of its patterns and creating a more hospitable space than the city itself.

The other issue arising from the above quote is the status of the subject, who is said to gain self-definition in relationship to such a striated whole. In contrast, the smooth space depicted in Kiefer's works locates us within conflicting scenarios that make personal identity problematic. This is one central result of the conception of tragic man, sketched in earlier chapters, and also of its Dionysian background. Vernant describes an important feature of Dionysian religion for our present consideration: the attempt of the initiates to gain intimate association with the god through the festivals does not give rise, he says, to any clear sense of personal identity. He asks:

> But is this fusion with the god a personal communion? It clearly is not. It is not to be reached in solitude, through meditation, prayer, and dialogue with an internal god, but in a group . . . using techniques of inducing collective hysteria, involving dancing, leaping, singing, and yelling, and wanderings that plunge a man deep into nature in the wild.[16]

Nature in the wild is distinctly different from nature ordered according to the principles of the striated grid. Unlike modern notions of identity, Dionysian fluidity is inconsistent with any notion of a centered individual self. The characteristic style of thought is more like the metaphorical thought of the Bwiti than that to which we are accustomed in the modern conception.

Since one source for our own ideas about the unity of nature and personal identity has been Western monotheism, we must remember that a different kind of religious outlook is likely to produce a different notion of human nature. Vernant argues, in fact, that it is crucial to remember that the "Greek gods are powers, not persons."[17] Although they are given names that seem to betoken personal essences, Vernant argues that they are not autonomous centers of thought and action. Rather, a "divine power . . . exists only by virtue of the network of relations that makes it part of the divine system as a whole."[18] Taking such a view seriously in the present moment of history would mean the displacement of human beings from the center of the world. Instead it points toward a more ambiguous basis for human existence that gives rise to no clear basis for identity. Such a consideration is particularly unwelcome within the world view of modernity, with its humanistic emphasis.

Kiefer, in fact, expresses his dissatisfaction with humanism when he disputes Beuys's view that humans stand at the middlepoint of the world. Kiefer says:

> It is not clear to me that we are the center of the world. We have talked about gods who are sad without humans. It could also be that there are gods who do not relate at all to human beings. As artists I believe it is possible to represent these powers. I know this is going to sound absurd when one says that man can perhaps perceive something or have a premonition of a power that has no relationship to him.[19]

If such powers are acknowledged even as possibilities, they undermine the basis for individual identity, which presupposes the orderly background of a rational world. Even when Kiefer portrays Jahweh's powers in the Exodus series, it is always through the hidden symbolism of lead blobs and other forms that obscure more than they show. As we expand our horizon into space, we may have to reconsider an encounter with these elemental forces.

Such a consideration may seem strange, given the intricate systems necessary to launch a ship into space. Why should we take seriously these throwbacks to the primitive just when total systems are the very means by which we venture into space? The space ship is a clear case of a simulation model, where the reality of the immediate environment gets defined by human need and desire. Yet Kiefer reminds us, as Kubrick did in *2001*, that these systems must function within a larger context where the forces at work may give us different results than we envision. The Dionysian background remains, whatever systems of control we may design. The pedagogical thrust in Kiefer's work helps to teach us of the continuing importance of this background even within our simulation systems.

Lyotard's analysis of the close relationship between modernity's world view and its socio-political system raises an additional question about Kiefer's version of the postmodern habitat, for it seems that if we embrace his tragic vision we may run the risk of undermining social and political safeguards associated with the concept of *liberal man*. The dangers associated with emphasis upon the collective have been all too evident in the twentieth century. What can be said to alleviate this concern? No simple answer is forthcoming, but it is important to observe that those who champion the ideals of liberal society may be guilty of self-deception. That is because the ideal of contract, which is supposed to govern so much of social and political life, falls under constraints imposed by capitalism. The idea of rationality that undergirds this contract ideal is, as Baudrillard has argued, compromised by its association with capitalism. He observes:

> Capital doesn't give a damn about the idea of the contract which is imputed to it—it is a monstrous, unprincipled undertaking, nothing more. Rather, it is "enlightened" thought which seeks to control capital by imposing rules on it. . . .
> Capital in fact has never been linked by a contract to the society it dominates. It is a sorcery of the social relation, it is a *challenge to society* and should be responded to as such. It is not a scandal to be denounced according to moral and economic rationality, but a challenge to take up according to symbolic law.[20]

That is why a return to the traditional ideals of liberal society seems limp in the face of collective forms of power. Contrary to such an approach, the challenge in the postmodern moment is to arrive at a new form of politics that can address the reality of the collective and better reflect the cultural complexities of the present age.

Where should we look for guidance in this situation? I have argued in earlier chapters that genealogical analysis will supply the key. Essential to such an approach is the recognition of how collective experience operates and how desires get shaped by social forces. In his introduction to Deleuze and Guattari's *Anti-Oedipus*, Mark Seem argues:

> Once we forget about our egos a non-neurotic form of politics becomes possible, where singularity and collectivity are no longer at odds with each other, and where collective expressions of desire are possible. Such a politics does not seek to regiment individuals according to a totalitarian system of norms, but to de-normalize and de-individualize through a multiplicity of new, collective arrangements against power. Its goal is the transformation of human relationships in a struggle against power.[21]

Rather than the politics of the grand narrative, which looks to political action to produce social progress, the politics of the little narrative envisions pluralistic goals and structures designed to prevent concentrations of power. Deleuze and Guattari cite Clastres's idea that the primitive tribe had deliberate mechanisms for warding off the concentration of power we take for granted in the modern state. They argue that within such a tribe:

> The chief is more like a leader or a star than a man of power, and is always in danger of being disavowed, abandoned by his people.
> But Clastres goes further, identifying *war* in primitive societies as the surest mechanism directed against the formation of the State: war maintains the dispersal and segmentarity of groups, and the warrior himself is caught in the process of accumulating exploits, a process which leads him on to solitude and a prestigious death, but without power.[22]

Nietzsche's frequent praise of the mentality of the warrior is presumably directed to the same point. Although the consequences of war today could hardly lead us to embrace this feature of archaic societies, we may think of taking specific measures against power as essential to the new politics. Whatever form it may take, collective politics cannot rely on the strategies that emphasize the rule of law and individual rights.

Baudrillard, for one, is skeptical even about a new form of politics, saying that there is an "impossibility of any politics" in our current situation.[23] Kiefer agrees to some extent, saying that "politics in itself is dead. Either politicians are actors or administrators."[24] That means that the hope for political solutions to our problems is slight. Baudrillard even describes his vision of the simulacrum as "transpolitical," because he thinks that the old political categories have lost their force.

> Power—Knowledge—Will—let the inventors of those ideas take responsibility for them. It makes perfect sense to me that the great masses, very snobbishly, delegate to the class of intellectuals, of politicians, this business of managing, of choosing, of knowing what one wants. They are joyously dumping all those burdensome categories that no one, deep down inside, really wants any part of. That people want to be told what they want is certainly not true; it is not clear either that they really want to know what they want, or that they desire to want at all. The whole edifice of socialism is based on that assumption. They start from the fact that this is what people ought to want, that they are social in the sense that they are supposed to know themselves, know what they want. I think we have pressed beyond that point.[25]

He means, of course, that the forces of the collective have finally produced identification only with the passing flux of the simulacrum, creating a population indifferent to established political purposes.

The question this raises is whether the cultural ideal of total systems has the effect of making us indifferent to desire and choice, and thereby establishes a new basis for human relations. While bourgeois ideology has built its account of human nature around the conflict of desire and reason, individual interest and the law, the social reality that accompanies the simulacrum may have no place for such a social drama. When we earlier considered Jameson's idea of the "death of the subject" in postmodern culture, we did not fully consider this possibility. However, our current concern with the larger habitat of postmodern life now makes that necessary. Jameson associated postmodern experience with the experience of schizophrenics, who find that the play of images and meanings pushes them away from any center. It is an "experience of limits beyond which you get dissolved."[26] This contrasts sharply with what was "*subjective* in the older sense that a personality is standing in front of the Alps and knowing the limits of the individual subject and the human ego."[27] Here, particularly, we must consider Kiefer's appeal to the natural habitat and his desire "to see where I am in eternity." We must ask whether this attitude expresses, after all, this sense of a subject standing before nature and knowing the limits of its own subjectivity. Is that the stance exhibited by his nature settings, or are we to understand it in different terms?

In replying to this question, we must recall that it is not the Romantic landscape that Kiefer gives us, but instead Theater of Cruelty landscapes staged to deconstruct our expectations. In making his appeal to ancient traditions within these settings, he is calling forth a view of nature closer to fate than to modernity's view. And we must remember, once more, that the modern subject is the counterpart of a particular view of nature. Kiefer's painting practice summons us toward an additional possibility, described by Jameson when he speaks of "a third possibility beyond the old bourgeois ego and the schizophrenic subject of our organization in society today: a *collective subject,* decentered but not schizophrenic."[28] Works like *Operation "Seelöwe"* (Plate I) make that appeal to the collective subject in quite explicit ways, but so do the cosmic landscapes, which transcend differences of nationality and special interest to appeal to the common condition of humanity in its collective venture into space.

These considerations fit with the analysis of desire and rationality provided in Chapter Four, where we considered Deleuze and Guattari's interpretation of desire and Jameson's emphasis upon the transition in postmodern thought from individual emotion to *intensities.* We remember Deleuze and Guattari's emphasis upon the way the socius inscribes desire with its structures of value. They argue that every society organizes and channels the operation of desire to produce collective goals, adding:

> When Nietzsche says that the selection is most often exerted *in favor of the large number,* he inaugurates a fundamental intuition that will inspire modern thought. For what he means is that the large numbers or the large aggregates do not exist prior to a selective pressure that might elicit singular lines from them, but that, quite on the contrary, these large numbers and aggregates are born of this selective pressure that crushes, eliminates, or regularizes the singularities.[29]

Just as Nietzsche reverses the priority modern thought gives to consciousness over language, so he also reverses the priority often given to language over cultural selection. Genealogical analysis, according to Deleuze and Guattari, shows that "selection does not presuppose a primary gregariousness; gregariousness presupposes the selection and is born of it. 'Culture' as a selective process of marking or inscription invents the large numbers in whose favor it is exerted." [30] These selective pressures inscribe desire with the form of the prevailing social milieu, making it clear why we find the simulacrum habitat described by Baudrillard and Jameson such a threat. If we were to have no other basis for desire, we would be in danger of becoming producers and consumers, and nothing else.

Yet genealogical analysis also shows the multiple strands emerging from history. They intersect and conflict, interact and divide, and in general provide the basis for a plurality of desires and interests beyond those having to do with productivity values. Although there may be tendencies of international capitalism to become the cultural dominant, as Jameson says, Kiefer displays other forces that still shape our habitat. His cosmic paintings remind us of the Dionysian ground of our earthly existence.

The *original representation* of reality in his works, contrasting with the forms of representation familiar within modernity, helps to remind us of our connection to the earth. These works express, with other contemporary examples, what Lucy Lippard has called "cultural overlay." [31] She examines a wide range of contemporary artists, from the land sculptures of Richard Long, who inscribes the landscape with traces of his own activities (such as walking), to the performance art of people like Dennis Oppenheim, who marks his own body and places himself at risk to display his connection to the earth. Lippard argues that these works establish common ground with people as far back as the Megalithic period, expressing the close relationship we continue to have with elemental nature. Lippard regards this dissemination of previous cultural attitudes as a healthy renewal of perceptions lost in the modern world. In particular, Lippard describes the interest of certain feminists in revitalizing our sense of the earth by their celebration of fertility,

birth and rebirth, and other phenomena we might describe as Dionysian. These postmodern developments, like Kiefer's own work,
seem to fulfill the injunction of Nietzsche's Zarathustra: "I entreat
you, my brothers, *remain true to the earth*." [32]

This teaching belongs at the center of contemporary debates
about the postmodern, since Baudrillard sees it as requiring that
we give up pretensions to rational order in favor of the seductions
that may attach to the play of images and to the changing forms
and connections that emerge within the simulacrum. Moreover,
Jameson's desire to arrive at cognitive maps of the world created
by multinational capitalism leads him, at times, to underrate the
importance of the earth. When he suggests that there is "a radical
eclipse of Nature itself" in postmodern culture, that may be only
historical observation, but it may, instead, be his recommendation
that we should forget nature and get on with creating our own
environment. Kiefer, on the other hand, clearly believes that the
setting of the earth is of unsurpassed importance for our contemporary consideration, at least as a symbol of our common grounding
and our hope for renewal.

The importance of our *image* of the human habitat can be seen if
we notice one other feature of Jameson's impressive analysis. In his
discussion of Louis Althusser's and Jacques Lacan's "redefinition of
ideology as 'the representation of the subject's *Imaginary* relationship to his or her *Real* conditions of existence,'" [33] he highlights
a role for imagination in cognitive mapping. We must be aware,
therefore, of the ideological role the modern image of nature has
played in supporting production. Yet to this image of nature, we
can oppose another as a counterweight: the symbolic picture of the
elemental forces represented by the earth.

Kiefer's works display a clear understanding of the interplay between different forms of imagination. All we need remember is the
transparent platform holding three chairs, hovering over the landscape in *Operation "Seelöwe,"* or the transparent pane of glass that
appears to transect the space between earth and sky in other works
like *The Red Sea* (Figure 33). This latter work, which transports the
Operation "Seelöwe" bathtub to the context of the Exodus, displays
the blood-red sea as if it were contained by a vessel, etched into the

landscape by someone's imagination. Born of Kiefer's own studio simulations, this painting focuses on the free play of images and meanings without subscribing to Baudrillard's euphoria in the face of an envisioned release of humanity from responsibility. Kiefer's consideration of imagination helps us to create cognitive maps to comprehend contemporary reality.

Kiefer's palpable grasp of the powers of imagination enables him to fulfill one pedagogical task of postmodern art: teaching us the importance of the habitat of the earth. His refusal to forget the consequences of war, the threat of nuclear destruction, and the negative outcomes of technology keeps being projected, in his Theater of Cruelty stagings, against the symbol of the earth. But even more than that, this artist brings fire to the earth, which purifies our vision of the abstract images of nature and history that stand at the root of so many of these consequences. His visionary sketch of the habitat for postmodern humans recalls us to the elemental relationship we have to the earth, to its place within the cosmos, and to previous human cultures who have understood, so well, the limits of human powers. This is the vision of tragic man.

PLATE I
Operation "Seelöwe,"
  1975
Unternehmen "Seelöwe"
Oil on canvas
220 × 300 cm
Collection of Norman
  Braman, Miami,
  Florida

PLATE II
Midgard, 1983–1985
Oil, acrylic,
  emulsion, shellac,
  straw, and singed
  spots on photo on
  canvas
270 × 280 cm
Collection Paul
  Maenz, Cologne

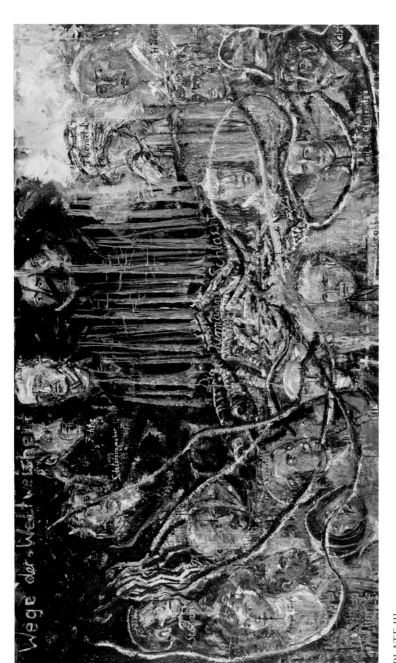

PLATE III
Ways of Worldly Wisdom, 1976–1977
Wege der Weltweisheit
Oil, acrylic, and shellac on burlap
305 × 500 cm
Collection Martijn Sanders, Amsterdam

PLATE IV
Johannisnacht,
    1978–1985
Acrylic, emulsion,
    and shellac on
    photo scraps on
    cardboard
66.5 × 75.5 cm
Collection of Eugene
    Stevens, Pepper
    Pike, Ohio

PLATE V
Yggdrasil, 1985
Acrylic, emulsion, shellac, and lead on
    photograph
103 × 83.5 cm
Collection of Stephen Frishberg,
    Philadelphia

PLATE VI
Midgard, 1980–1985
Oil, acrylic, emulsion, and shellac on photograph and canvas
360 × 604 cm
The Carnegie Museum, Pittsburgh

PLATE VII
Cherubim, Seraphim,
1983
Oil, acrylic,
emulsion, shellac,
straw, and
xylograph
fragments on
canvas
288 × 340 cm
Nationalgalerie,
Berlin

PLATE VIII
Parsifal II, 1973
Oil on oatmeal wallpaper on gray cotton
300 × 533 cm
Kunsthaus Zurich

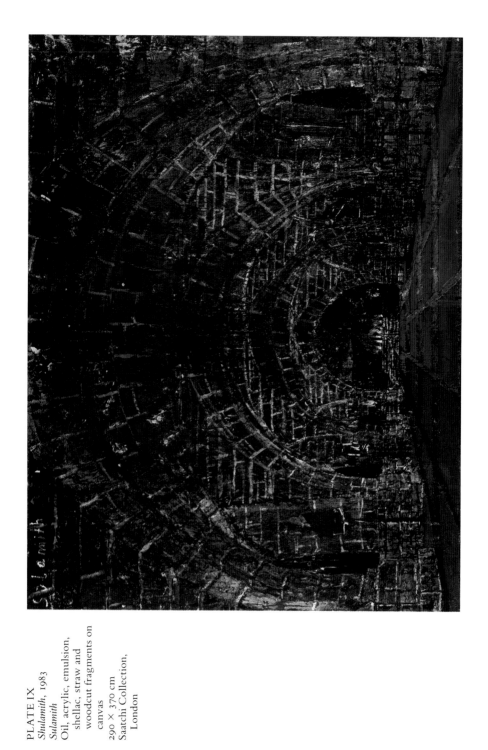

PLATE IX
Shulamith, 1983
Sulamith
Oil, acrylic, emulsion,
shellac, straw and
woodcut fragments on
canvas
290 × 370 cm
Saatchi Collection,
London

PLATE X
Emanation, 1984–1986
Oil, acrylic, and emulsion on canvas; applied lead tongue and photographs
410 × 280 cm
Walker Art Center, Minneapolis

PLATE XI
Wayland's Song (with
Wing), 1982
Wölundlied (mit Flügel)
Lead object and lead
  strips mounted on oil,
  emulsion, and straw on
  canvas
280 × 380 cm
Saatchi Collection,
  London

Notes
Bibliography
Index

Notes

INTRODUCTION

1. Donald Kuspit, "Flak from the 'Radicals': The American Case Against Current German Painting," in Jack Cowart, ed., *Expressions: New Art from Germany* (St. Louis: St. Louis Art Museum, 1983), p. 44.

2. Clement Greenberg, "Modernist Painting," in Francis Frascina and Charles Harrison, eds., *Modern Art and Modernism* (New York: Harper and Row, 1982), pp. 6–7. Greenberg says more generally that "visual art should confine itself exclusively to what is given in visual experience, and make no reference to anything given in other orders of experience" (p. 8).

3. Ibid., p. 8.

4. *Anselm Kiefer* (Düsseldorf: Städtische Kuntshalle; Paris: ARC/ Musée d'Art Moderne de la Ville de Paris; Jerusalem: Israel Museum, 1984), p. 62. Hereafter referred to as *Anselm Kiefer* (1984 catalog).

5. Peter Bürger, *Theory of the Avant-Garde*, trans. Michael Shaw (Minneapolis: University of Minnesota Press, 1984). The ideas discussed here appear primarily between pp. 16 and 24.

6. Ibid., pp. 60–63.

7. Ibid., p. 31.

8. Greenberg, "Modernist Painting," p. 9. Although Greenberg says that this convergence is accidental "from the point of view of art itself" (pp. 8–9), his analysis shows that it is far from accidental.

9. Ibid., p. 8.

CHAPTER ONE

1. Michel Foucault, *The Order of Things: An Archaeology of the Human Sciences* (London: Tavistock Publications, 1974), pp. 17–30.

2. Friedrich Nietzsche, *The Gay Science*, trans. Walter Kaufmann (New York: Random House, 1974), para. 125.

3. Ibid.

4. Foucault, *Order of Things*, p. 62.

5. Ibid., pp. 56–58.

6. Herbert Butterfield, *The Origins of Modern Science, 1300–1800* (rev. ed.; New York: Free Press, 1965), pp. 77–78.

7. Foucault, *Order of Things*, pp. 59–61.

8. John C. Gilmour, *Picturing the World* (Albany, N.Y.: SUNY Press, 1986). See especially chaps. 4 and 5 for this argument.

9. Rudolf Arnheim, *The Power of the Center: A Study of Composition in the Visual Arts* (Berkeley: University of California Press, 1982), pp. vii–ix.

10. Ibid., pp. 2–3.

11. Ibid., p. 1.

12. Martin Heidegger, "The Age of the World Picture," *The Question Concerning Technology and Other Essays*, trans. William Lovitt (New York: Harper and Row, 1977), pp. 126–127. Heidegger adds later: "The fundamental event of the modern age is the conquest of the world as picture. The word 'picture' [*Bild*] now means the structured image [*Gebild*] that is the creature of man's producing which represents and sets before. In such producing, man contends for the position in which he can be that particular being who gives the measure and draws up the guidelines for everything that is" (p. 134).

13. Such a position is taken by Suzi Gablik, *Progress in Art* (New York: Rizzoli International Publications, 1977). See especially chap. 5.

14. Foucault, *Order of Things*, p. 79.

15. Ibid., p. 78.

16. Ibid., p. 62.

17. Ibid.

18. Rosalind E. Krauss, *The Originality of the Avant-Garde and Other Modernist Myths* (Cambridge, Mass.: MIT Press, 1985), pp. 9–22.

19. Kandinsky takes this position in his influential book, *Concerning the Spiritual in Art*, trans. M. T. H. Sadler (New York: Dover, 1977). Mondrian once said, "If one does not represent things, a place remains for the Divine" (quoted by Robert Welsh in "Mondrian and Theosophy," *Piet Mondrian Centennial Exhibition* [New York: Solomon R. Guggenheim Museum, 1971], p. 50).

20. Krauss, *Originality of the Avant-Garde*, p. 9.

21. Ibid., p. 10.

22. Ibid., pp. 18–19.

23. Ibid., pp. 157–160.

24. Berthold Hinz, *Art in the Third Reich*, trans. Robert Kimber and

Rita Kimber (Oxford, Eng.: Basil Blackwell, 1979), p. 190. See also pp. 148–149.

25. Krauss, *Originality of the Avant-Garde*, p. 121.

26. Ibid., p. 13.

27. Ibid., p. 4.

28. Douglas Crimp, "On the Museum's Ruins," in Hal Foster, ed., *The Anti-Aesthetic: Essays in Postmodern Culture* (Port Townsend, Wash.: Bay Press, 1983), p. 53. Crimp is speaking of Rauschenberg's art in this passage.

CHAPTER TWO

1. Gudrun Inboden, "Exodus from Historical Time," in Paul Maenz and Gerd de Vries, eds., *Anselm Kiefer* (Köln: Galerie Paul Maenz, 1986), pp. 14–15.

2. Michel Foucault, *The Order of Things: An Archaeology of the Human Sciences* (London: Tavistock Publications, 1974), p. 304.

3. Jean Baudrillard, *The Mirror of Production*, trans. Mark Poster (St. Louis: Telos Press, 1975), p. 53.

4. Ibid., pp. 53–54.

5. Friedrich Nietzsche, *Thus Spoke Zarathustra*, trans. R. J. Hollingdale (reprint; New York: Penguin Books, 1969), p. 161.

6. Friedrich Nietzsche, *Twilight of the Idols*, trans. R. J. Hollingdale (reprint; New York: Penguin Books, 1977), p. 39.

7. Jean Baudrillard, *Simulations*, trans. Paul Foss, Paul Patton, and Philip Beitchman (New York: Semiotext[e], 1983), p. 8.

8. Ibid., p. 9.

9. Gilles Deleuze, "Plato and the Simulacrum," trans. Rosalind Krauss, *October* 27 (Winter, 1983): 47–48.

10. Ibid., p. 46.

11. Ibid., p. 47.

12. Baudrillard, *Simulations*, p. 2.

13. Ibid., p. 3.

14. Baudrillard, *Mirror of Production*, p. 19.

15. Peter Bürger, *Theory of the Avant-Garde*, trans. Michael Shaw (Minneapolis: University of Minnesota Press, 1984), pp. 60–61.

16. Ibid., p. 61.

17. Baudrillard, *Mirror of Production*, p. 20.

18. Baudrillard, *Simulations*, pp. 96–97.

19. Jürgen Habermas, "Modernity—an Incomplete Project," in Hal Foster, ed., *The Anti-Aesthetic: Essays in Postmodern Culture* (Port Townsend, Wash.: Bay Press, 1983), pp. 3–15.

20. Baudrillard, *Mirror of Production*, pp. 32–33.

21. Ibid., p. 102.

22. Ibid., p. 82.

23. Ibid., p. 94.

24. Ibid., p. 98. For further discussion of symbolic exchange see Marcel Mauss, *The Gift: Forms and Functions of Exchange in Archaic Societies*, trans. Ian Cunnison (Glencoe, Ill.: Free Press, 1954).

25. Baudrillard, *Simulations*, p. 12.

26. Martin Heidegger, "Building Dwelling Thinking," *Poetry, Language, Thought*, trans. and ed. Albert Hofstadter (New York: Harper and Row, 1971), pp. 149–151.

CHAPTER THREE

1. See Jacques Derrida, "The Theater of Cruelty and the Closure of Representation," *Writing and Difference*, trans. Alan Bass (reprint; London: Routledge and Kegan Paul, 1985), p. 238.

2. Antonin Artaud, *The Theater and Its Double*, trans. Mary Caroline Richards (New York: Grove Press, 1958), p. 109.

3. Friedrich Nietzsche, *The Will to Power*, ed. Walter Kaufmann, trans. Walter Kaufmann and R. J. Hollingdale (reprint; New York: Random House, 1968), para. 1067.

4. Ibid.

5. *Anselm Kiefer* (1984 catalog), p. 132. The original reference may be found in St. Dionysius the Areopagite, *The Celestial and Ecclesiastical Hierarchy*, trans. Rev. John Parker (London: Skeffington and Son, 1894).

6. Anne Seymour, "Notes on the Plates," in *Anselm Kiefer Watercolours, 1970–1982* (London: Anthony d'Offay Gallery, 1983), plate 13.

7. Walter Benjamin, "The Work of Art in the Age of Mechanical Reproduction," in Hannah Arendt, ed., *Illuminations*, trans. Harry Zohn (reprint; New York: Schocken Books, 1969), pp. 218–222.

8. *Anselm Kiefer* (1984 catalog), p. 30.

9. Derrida, "La Parole Soufflée," *Writing and Difference*, p. 185.

10. Ibid., p. 235.

11. Artaud, *Theater and Its Double*, p. 10.

12. Ibid., p. 11.

13. Ibid., p. 60.

14. Friedrich Nietzsche, *Beyond Good and Evil*, trans. R. J. Hollingdale (reprint; New York: Penguin Books, 1981), para. 229.

15. Friedrich Nietzsche, *The Birth of Tragedy*, trans. Walter Kaufmann (New York: Random House, 1967), pp. 34–35.

16. Ibid., pp. 39–40.

17. Ibid., p. 61.

18. Derrida, "Theater of Cruelty," p. 237.

19. Martin Heidegger, "Building Dwelling Thinking," *Poetry, Language, Thought*, trans. and ed. Albert Hofstadter (New York: Harper and Row, 1971), p. 157.

20. Jacques Derrida, *The Truth in Painting*, trans. Geoff Bennington and Ian McLeod (Chicago: University of Chicago Press, 1987), p. 318.

21. Gudrun Inboden, "Exodus from Historical Time," in Paul Maenz and Gerd de Vries, eds., *Anselm Kiefer*, (Köln: Galerie Paul Maenz, 1986), p. 5.

22. Benjamin, "Work of Art," p. 236.

23. Jacques Derrida, "Differance," *Speech and Phenomena*, trans. David B. Allison (Evanston, Ill.: Northwestern University Press, 1973), p. 138.

24. Ibid., pp. 142–143.

25. Jean-Pierre Vernant and Pierre Vidal-Naquet, *Tragedy and Myth in Ancient Greece*, trans. Janet Lloyd (Atlantic Highlands, N.J.: Humanities Press, 1981), p. 4.

26. Jean-Pierre Vernant, *Myth and Thought Among the Ancient Greeks* (Boston: Routledge and Kegan Paul, 1983), p. 325.

27. Vernant and Vidal-Naquet, *Tragedy and Myth*, p. 18.

28. Nietzsche, *Beyond Good and Evil*, para. 19.

29. Ibid.

30. Vernant and Vidal-Naquet, *Tragedy and Myth*, p. 40.

31. Artaud, *Theater and Its Double*, p. 12.

32. Vernant and Vidal-Naquet, *Tragedy and Myth*, pp. 12–13.

33. Ibid., p. 13.

CHAPTER FOUR

1. Victor Burgin, *The End of Art Theory: Criticism and Postmodernity* (London: Macmillan, 1986), p. 41.

2. This is reported by Mark Rosenthal from an interview with Kiefer. See Mark Rosenthal, ed., *Anselm Kiefer* (Chicago: Art Institute; Philadelphia: Philadelphia Museum of Art, 1987), p. 51.

3. Fredric Jameson, "Postmodernism and Consumer Society," in Hal Foster, ed., *The Anti-Aesthetic: Essays in Postmodern Culture* (Port Townsend, Wash.: Bay Press, 1983), p. 114.

4. Rosalind Krauss, *The Originality of the Avant-Garde and Other Modernist Myths* (Cambridge, Mass.: MIT Press, 1985), p. 34.

5. Reported in Steven Henry Madoff, "Anselm Kiefer: A Call to Memory," *Art News* 86, no. 8 (1987): 128.

6. Michael Fried, "Three American Painters," in Francis Frascina and Charles Harrison, eds., *Modern Art and Modernism: A Critical Anthology* (London: Harper and Row, 1982), p. 120.

7. Fredric Jameson, "Postmodernism, or the Cultural Logic of Late Capitalism," *New Left Review* 146 (1984): 63.

8. Burgin, *End of Art Theory*, p. 49.

9. Friedrich Nietzsche, *The Gay Science*, trans. Walter Kaufmann (New York: Random House, 1974), para. 354.

10. Ibid.

11. Rosenthal, ed., *Anselm Kiefer*, p. 60.

12. Ibid., p. 32.

13. Anne Seymour, "Notes on the Plates," *Anselm Kiefer Watercolours, 1970–1982* (London: Anthony d'Offay Gallery, 1983), plate 21.

14. Friedrich Nietzsche, *Twilight of the Idols*, trans. R. J. Hollingdale (reprint; New York: Penguin Books, 1977), p. 33.

15. Ibid., p. 35.

16. Leo Steinberg, *Other Criteria: Confrontations with Twentieth Century Art* (New York: Oxford University Press, 1972), p. 82.

17. Ibid., p. 88.

18. Ibid.

19. Rudolf Arnheim, *The Genesis of a Painting: Picasso's Guernica* (Berkeley: University of California Press, 1962), p. 9.

20. Ibid., p. 28.

21. Madoff, "Anselm Kiefer," p. 126.

22. Friedrich Nietzsche, *Beyond Good and Evil*, trans. R. J. Hollingdale (reprint; New York: Penguin Books, 1981), para. 36.

23. Pierre Klossowski, "Nietzsche's Experience of the Eternal Return," in David B. Allison, ed., *The New Nietzsche* (New York: Dell Publishing Co., 1977), p. 111.

24. Paul Celan, "Fugue of Death," trans. Christopher Middleton, in Charles Tomlinson, ed., *The Oxford Book of Verse in English Translation* (Oxford, Eng.: Oxford University Press, 1980), no. 564.

25. For discussion of this work see Rosenthal, ed., *Anselm Kiefer*, pp. 115–119.

26. Jameson, "Postmodernism, or the Cultural Logic of Late Capitalism," p. 62.

27. Jacques Derrida, "The Theater of Cruelty and the Closure of Representation," *Writing and Difference*, trans. Alan Bass (London: Routledge and Kegan Paul, 1985), p. 238.

28. Reported in Madoff, "Anselm Kiefer," p. 130.

29. Martin Heidegger, *The Will to Power as Art*, vol. 1 of *Nietzsche*, trans. David Farrell Krell (San Francisco: Harper and Row, 1979), p. 51.

30. Ibid., p. 49.

31. Jameson, "Postmodernism, or the Cultural Logic of Late Capitalism," p. 64.

32. Madoff, "Anselm Kiefer," p. 128.

CHAPTER FIVE

1. G. W. F. Hegel, *Reason in History: A General Introduction to the Philosophy of History*, trans. Robert S. Hartman (Indianapolis, Ind.: Bobbs-Merrill, 1953), p. 13.

2. Jean François Lyotard, *The Postmodern Condition: A Report on Knowledge*, trans. Geoff Bennington and Brian Massumi (Manchester, Eng.: Manchester University Press, 1984), p. 27.

3. Lyotard characterizes realism within art as concerned with preserving "various consciousnesses from doubt. Industrial photography and cinema will be superior to painting and the novel whenever the objective is to stabilize the referent, to arrange it according to a point of view which endows it with a recognizable meaning, to reproduce the syntax and vocabulary which enable the addressee to decipher images and sequences quickly, and so to arrive easily at the consciousness of his own identity" (ibid., p. 74).

4. Friedrich Nietzsche, *Twilight of the Idols*, trans. R. J. Hollingdale (reprint; New York: Penguin Books, 1977), p. 86.

5. Friedrich Nietzsche, *The Birth of Tragedy*, trans. Walter Kaufmann (New York: Random House, 1967), p. 75.

6. Gilles Deleuze and Félix Guattari, *Anti-Oedipus: Capitalism and Schizophrenia*, trans. Robert Hurley, Mark Seem, and Helen R. Lane (Minneapolis: University of Minnesota Press, 1983), p. 142.

7. Ibid., p. 144.

8. Jean-Pierre Vernant, *Myth and Thought Among the Ancient Greeks* (Boston: Routledge and Kegan Paul, 1983), p. 79.

9. Mark Rosenthal, ed., *Anselm Kiefer* (Chicago: Art Institute; Philadelphia: Philadelphia Museum of Art, 1987), p. 138. See also the discussion of this by Gudrun Inboden in Paul Maenz and Gerd de Vries, eds., *Anselm Kiefer* (Köln: Galerie Paul Maenz, 1986), p. 14.

10. Vernant, *Myth and Thought*, p. 333.

11. Jean-Pierre Vernant and Pierre Vidal-Naquet, *Tragedy and Myth in Ancient Greece*, trans. Janet Lloyd (Atlantic Highlands, N.J.: Humanities Press, 1981), p. 21.

12. Ibid., p. 13.

13. On the snake image in Old Europe see Marija Gimbutas, *The Goddesses and Gods of Old Europe* (reprint; Berkeley: University of California Press, 1982), pp. 93–101. For discussion of the snake in shamanism, see Mircea Eliade, *Shamanism: Archaic Techniques of Ecstasy*, trans. Willard R. Trask (Princeton, N.J.: Princeton University Press, 1972).

14. Lyotard, *Postmodern Condition*, p. 18.

15. Ibid.

16. Ibid., p. 29.

17. Ibid., p. 30.

18. Ibid., p. 31.

19. Friedrich Nietzsche, *Thus Spoke Zarathustra*, trans. R. J. Hollingdale (reprint; New York: Penguin Books, 1969), p. 65.

20. Nietzsche, *Twilight of the Idols*, p. 50.

21. Reported in Rosenthal, ed., *Anselm Kiefer*, p. 17.

22. Lyotard, *Postmodern Condition*, p. 15.

23. For discussion of this issue see an excellent article by Joseph Margolis, "Reinterpreting Interpretation," *Journal of Aesthetics and Art Criticism* 47, no. 3 (Summer, 1989): 238–239.

24. Lyotard, *Postmodern Condition*, pp. 20–21.

25. James W. Fernandez, *Bwiti: An Ethnography of the Religious Imagination in Africa* (Princeton, N.J.: Princeton University Press, 1982). See especially chaps. 19–20.

26. Ibid., pp. 506, 514, 520, and 525.

27. Ibid., pp. 527–528.

28. James W. Fernandez, *Persuasions and Performances: The Play of Tropes*

in Culture (Bloomington: Indiana University Press, 1986), p. 183. For general discussion of the sermonizing and its relation to the hearer, see chap. 7, "Edification by Puzzlement."

29. Fernandez, *Bwiti*, p. 503.

30. Lyotard, *Postmodern Condition*, p. 21.

31. Ibid., p. 22. A similar point is made by Vernant concerning the ancient bards. He says that "the rules of oral composition themselves insist that the bard should have at his command not only a whole body of themes and tales, but also a technique of formulaic diction which comes to him, ready-made, and which involves the use of traditional expressions, predetermined combinations of words, and established rules of verification" (Vernant, *Myth and Thought*, p. 77).

32. Lyotard, *Postmodern Condition*, p. 22.

33. Ibid.

34. Ibid., p. 37.

35. Ibid., p. 40.

CHAPTER SIX

1. Reported in Steven Henry Madoff, "Anselm Kiefer: A Call to Memory," *Art News* 86, no. 8 (1987): 129.

2. Friedrich Nietzsche, *Thus Spoke Zarathustra*, trans. R. J. Hollingdale (reprint; New York: Penguin Books, 1969), p. 178.

3. Ibid.

4. Ibid., p. 179.

5. Ibid., p. 42.

6. Gilles Deleuze and Félix Guattari, *Anti-Oedipus: Capitalism and Schizophrenia*, trans. Robert Hurley, Mark Seem, and Helen R. Lane (Minneapolis: University of Minnesota Press, 1983), p. 154.

7. Ibid.

8. Ibid., pp. 154–166.

9. Ibid., p. 29.

10. Ibid., p. 154.

11. Ibid., pp. 32–33.

12. The source for this myth is "The Lay of Volund [Wayland]," *The Poetic Edda*, trans. L. M. Hollander (2nd ed.; Austin: University of Texas, 1962), pp. 159–167.

13. For *Baum mit Flügel* (Tree with Wing; 1979), see Jack Cowart, ed., *Expressions: New Art from Germany* (St. Louis: St. Louis Art Museum,

1983), p. 112. For *Baum mit Palette* (Tree with Palette; 1978), see *Art of Our Time: The Saatchi Collection, No. 3* (New York: Rizzoli Publications, 1984), plate 30.

14. He does so, for example, in *The Painter's Guardian Angel* (1975), *Icarus* (1981), and *Mount Olivet* (1980).

15. *Anselm Kiefer* (1984 catalog), p. 102.

16. Mircea Eliade, *The Forge and the Crucible* (2nd ed.; Chicago: University of Chicago Press, 1978), pp. 43–52.

17. Ibid., p. 8.

18. Mircea Eliade, *Shamanism: Archaic Techniques of Ecstasy*, trans. Willard R. Trask (Princeton, N.J.: Princeton University Press, 1972), chap. 13, "Parallel Myths, Symbols, and Rites," pp. 478–479.

19. Ibid., pp. 483–484.

20. Eliade, *The Forge and the Crucible*, p. 79.

21. Ibid., p. 31.

22. Anne Seymour, "Notes on the Plates," in *Anselm Kiefer Watercolours, 1970–1982* (London: Anthony d'Offay Gallery, 1983), note to plate 21.

23. Ibid.

24. Eliade, *The Forge and the Crucible*, p. 173.

25. Artaud uses this phrase as the title for one essay. See Antonin Artaud, *The Theater and Its Double*, trans. Mary Caroline Richards (New York: Grove Press, 1958), pp. 48–52.

26. Ibid., p. 48. Bettina L. Knapp, in describing the purposes of the alchemist, says: "Although the techniques used by the alchemists varied, they had a common goal: to divest the baser elements with which they were working of their impurities by means of a series of experiments which they hoped would take them from primal unity to the creation of the Philosopher's Stone" (*Theater and Alchemy* [Detroit: Wayne State University Press, 1980], p. 5).

27. See Mark Rosenthal's discussion of this painting in Mark Rosenthal, ed., *Anselm Kiefer* (Chicago: Art Institute; Philadelphia: Philadelphia Museum of Art, 1987), p. 143.

28. Artaud, *Theater and Its Double*, p. 51.

29. Eliade, *The Forge and the Crucible*, p. 153.

30. Knapp, *Theater and Alchemy*, p. 9.

31. For discussion of the meaning of this symbolism, see Eliade, *The Forge and the Crucible*, where he writes: "We must emphasize the importance accorded by the alchemists to the 'terrible' and 'sinister' experiences of 'blackness', of spiritual death, of descent into hell" (p. 161); or "The phase which follows the *nigredo,* that is, the 'work in white', the *leukosis,*

the *albedo*, probably corresponds, on the spiritual plane, to a resurrection expressed by the assumption of certain states of consciousness inaccessible to the uninitiated" (p. 162).

32. Knapp, *Theater and Alchemy*, p. 9.

33. Mircea Eliade, *Myth and Reality*, trans. Willard R. Trask (reprint; New York: Harper and Row, 1975), p. 5.

34. Ibid.

35. Ibid., p. 11.

36. Friedrich Nietzsche, *On The Genealogy of Morals*, trans. Walter Kaufmann and R. J. Hollingdale (New York: Random House, 1967), pt. 2, sec. 4.

37. Friedrich Nietzsche, *The Gay Science*, trans. Walter Kaufmann (New York: Random House, 1974), par. 354.

38. Eliade, *Myth and Reality*, p. 13.

PART III INTRODUCTION

1. Jacqueline Burckhardt, ed., *Ein Gespräch: Joseph Beuys, Jannis Kounellis, Anselm Kiefer, and Enzo Cucchi* (Zürich: PARKETT-Verlag, 1986), p. 157.

2. Ibid., p. 119.

3. Jean Baudrillard, *The Mirror of Production*, trans. Mark Poster (St. Louis: Telos Press, 1975), pp. 32–33.

4. Burckhardt, ed., *Ein Gespräch*, p. 69.

5. Ibid., p. 114.

CHAPTER SEVEN

1. Jean-François Lyotard, *The Postmodern Condition: A Report on Knowledge*, trans. Geoff Bennington and Brian Massumi (Manchester, Eng.: Manchester University Press, 1984), p. 81.

2. Jacqueline Burckhardt, ed., *Ein Gespräch: Joseph Beuys, Jannis Kounellis, Anselm Kiefer, and Enzo Cucchi* (Zürich: PARKETT-Verlag, 1986), p. 12.

3. Jürgen Habermas, "Modernity—an Incomplete Project," in Hal Foster, ed., *The Anti-Aesthetic: Essays in Postmodern Culture* (Port Townsend, Wash.: Bay Press, 1983), p. 9.

4. Ibid., p. 8.

5. Ibid., pp. 9–10.

6. Ibid., p. 14.

7. Lyotard, *Postmodern Condition*, p. 43.

8. Ibid.

9. Ibid., p. 82.

10. Ibid., p. 60.

11. Antonin Artaud, *The Theater and Its Double*, trans. Mary Caroline Richards (New York: Grove Press, 1958), p. 109.

12. Lyotard, *Postmodern Condition*, p. 44.

13. Ibid., p. 45.

14. Fredric Jameson, "Postmodernism, or the Cultural Logic of Late Capitalism," *New Left Review* 146 (1984): 79–80.

15. Martin Heidegger, "The Question Concerning Technology," *The Question Concerning Technology and Other Essays*, trans. William Lovitt (New York: Harper and Row, 1977), p. 4.

16. Martin Heidegger, "What Are Poets For?," *Poetry, Language, Thought*, trans. and ed. Albert Hofstadter (New York: Harper and Row, 1971), p. 111.

17. Jean Baudrillard, *The Mirror of Production*, trans. Mark Poster (St. Louis: Telos Press, 1975), pp. 53–54. Baudrillard adds: "Nature appeared truly as an essence in all its glory but under the sign of the *principle of production*. This separation also involves the *principle of signification*. Under the objective stamp of Science, Technology, and Production, Nature becomes the great Signified, the great Referent. It is ideally charged with 'reality'; it becomes *the* Reality, expressible by a process that is always somehow a process of labor, at once *transformation* and *transcription*. Its 'reality' principle is this operational principle of an industrial structuration and a significative pattern" (ibid., p. 54).

18. Martin Heidegger, "The Age of the World Picture," *The Question Concerning Technology and Other Essays*, trans. William Lovitt (New York: Harper and Row, 1977), p. 131.

19. Baudrillard, *Mirror of Production*, p. 55.

20. Ibid., p. 56.

21. Ibid., pp. 58–59.

22. Ibid., p. 64.

23. Ibid., p. 69.

24. Ibid., pp. 78–79.

25. Ibid., pp. 82–83.

26. Heidegger, "Question Concerning Technology," pp. 19–23.

27. Ibid., p. 14.

28. Gilles Deleuze and Félix Guattari, *Nomadology: The War Machine*, trans. Brian Massumi (New York: Semiotext[e], 1986), p. 22. Also in Deleuze and Guattari, *A Thousand Plateaus*, trans. Brian Massumi (Minneapolis: University of Minnesota Press, 1987).

29. Ibid., pp. 102–103.

30. Heidegger, "Question Concerning Technology," p. 17.

31. Burckhardt, ed., *Ein Gespräch*, p. 131.

32. Ibid., p. 112.

33. Heidegger, "Question Concerning Technology," p. 35.

34. Lyotard, *Postmodern Condition*, p. 61.

35. Joseph Margolis, "Reinterpreting Interpretation," *Journal of Aesthetics and Art Criticism* 47, no. 3 (Summer, 1989): 245.

36. Lyotard, *Postmodern Condition*, p. 61.

37. Burckhardt, ed., *Ein Gespräch*, p. 54.

CHAPTER EIGHT

1. Jean Baudrillard, *The Mirror of Production*, trans. Mark Poster (St. Louis: Telos Press, 1975), p. 98.

2. Ibid., p. 102.

3. Jean Baudrillard, *Forget Foucault* (New York: Semiotext[e], 1987), p. 84.

4. Jean Baudrillard, "The Ecstasy of Communication," in Hal Foster, ed., *The Anti-Aesthetic: Essays in Postmodern Culture* (Port Townsend, Wash.: Bay Press, 1983), p. 128.

5. Fredric Jameson, "Postmodernism, or the Cultural Logic of Late Capitalism," *New Left Review* 146 (1984): 66.

6. Jean Baudrillard, *Simulations*, trans. Paul Foss, Paul Patton, and Philip Beitchman (New York: Semiotext[e], 1983), p. 2.

7. Ibid., p. 3.

8. Ibid., p. 50.

9. Baudrillard, *Forget Foucault*, p. 77.

10. Jameson, "Postmodernism, or the Cultural Logic of Late Capitalism," p. 71.

11. Ibid., p. 77.

12. Ibid., p. 89.

13. Ibid., p. 81.

14. Gilles Deleuze and Félix Guattari, *Nomadology: The War Machine*, trans. Brian Massumi (New York: Semiotext[e], 1986), pp. 47–48.

15. Jameson, "Postmodernism, or the Cultural Logic of Late Capitalism," p. 81.

16. Jean-Pierre Vernant, *Myth and Thought Among the Ancient Greeks* (Boston: Routledge and Kegan Paul, 1983), p. 325.

17. Ibid., p. 328.

18. Ibid., p. 329.

19. Jacqueline Burckhardt, ed., *Ein Gespräch: Joseph Beuys, Jannis Kounellis, Anselm Kiefer, and Enzo Cucchi* (Zürich: PARKETT-Verlag, 1986), p. 113.

20. Baudrillard, *Simulations*, pp. 29–30.

21. Gilles Deleuze and Félix Guattari, *Anti-Oedipus: Capitalism and Schizophrenia*, trans. Robert Hurley, Mark Seem, and Helen R. Lane (Minneapolis: University of Minnesota Press, 1983), p. xxi.

22. Deleuze and Guattari, *Nomadology*, p. 11.

23. Baudrillard, *Forget Foucault*, p. 98.

24. Burckhardt, ed., *Ein Gespräch*, p. 59.

25. Baudrillard, *Forget Foucault*, pp. 103–104.

26. Quoted in Anders Stephanson, "Interview with Fredric Jameson," *Flash Art* 131 (December, 1986/January, 1987): 69.

27. Ibid.

28. Ibid., p. 70.

29. Deleuze and Guattari, *Anti-Oedipus*, pp. 342–343.

30. Ibid., p. 343.

31. Lucy R. Lippard, *Overlay: Contemporary Art and the Art of Prehistory* (New York: Pantheon Books, 1983).

32. Friedrich Nietzsche, *Thus Spoke Zarathustra*, trans. R. J. Hollingdale (reprint; New York: Penguin Books, 1969), p. 42.

33. Jameson, "Postmodernism, or the Cultural Logic of Late Capitalism," p. 90.

Bibliography

Anselm Kiefer. Düsseldorf: Städtische Kuntshalle; Paris: ARC/Musée d'Art Moderne de la Ville de Paris; Jerusalem: Israel Museum, 1984.

Anselm Kiefer: Departure from Egypt, 1984–1985. New York: Marian Goodman Gallery, 1985.

Anselm Kiefer Watercolours, 1970–1982. London: Anthony d'Offay Gallery, 1983.

Arnheim, Rudolf. *The Genesis of a Painting: Picasso's Guernica.* Berkeley: University of California Press, 1962.

———. *The Power of the Center: A Study of Composition in the Visual Arts.* Berkeley: University of California Press, 1982.

Art of Our Time: The Saatchi Collection, No. 3. New York: Rizzoli International Publications, 1984.

Artaud, Antonin. *The Theater and Its Double,* trans. Mary Caroline Richards. New York: Grove Press, 1958.

Baudrillard, Jean. *Forget Foucault.* New York: Semiotext[e], 1987.

———. *The Mirror of Production,* trans. Mark Poster. St. Louis: Telos Press, 1975.

———. *Simulations,* trans. Paul Foss, Paul Patton, and Philip Beitchman. New York: Semiotext[e], 1983.

Benjamin, Walter. "The Work of Art in the Age of Mechanical Reproduction." In Hannah Arendt, ed., *Illuminations,* trans. Harry Zohn. New York: Schocken Books, 1969.

Burckhardt, Jacqueline, ed. *Ein Gespräch: Joseph Beuys, Jannis Kounellis, Anselm Kiefer, and Enzo Cucchi.* Zürich: PARKETT-Verlag, 1986.

Bürger, Peter. *Theory of the Avant-Garde,* trans. Michael Shaw. Minneapolis: University of Minnesota Press, 1984.

Burgin, Victor. *The End of Art Theory: Criticism and Postmodernity.* London: Macmillan, 1986.

Butterfield, Herbert. *The Origins of Modern Science, 1300–1800.* Rev. ed.; New York: Free Press, 1965.

Celan, Paul. "Fugue of Death," trans. Christopher Middleton. In Charles

Tomlinson, ed., *The Oxford Book of Verse in English Translation.* Oxford, Eng.: Oxford University Press, 1980.

Cowart, Jack, ed. *Expressions: New Art from Germany.* St. Louis: St. Louis Art Museum, 1983.

Crimp, Douglas. "On the Museum's Ruins." In Hal Foster, ed., *The Anti-Aesthetic: Essays on Postmodern Culture.* Port Townsend, Wash.: Bay Press, 1983.

Deleuze, Gilles. *Nietzsche and Philosophy,* trans. Hugh Tomlinson. New York: Columbia University Press, 1983.

———. "Plato and the Simulacrum," trans. Rosalind Krauss. *October* 27 (winter, 1983): 45–56.

Deleuze, Gilles, and Félix Guattari. *Anti-Oedipus: Capitalism and Schizophrenia,* trans. Robert Hurley, Mark Seem, and Helen R. Lane. Minneapolis: University of Minnesota Press, 1983.

———. *Nomadology: The War Machine,* trans. Brian Massumi. New York: Semiotext[e], 1986. Reprinted in Deleuze and Guattari, *A Thousand Plateaus: Capitalism and Schizophrenia,* trans. Brian Massumi. Minneapolis: University of Minnesota Press, 1987.

Derrida, Jacques. "Differance." In Derrida, *Speech and Phenomena,* trans. David B. Allison. Evanston, Ill.: Northwestern University Press, 1973.

———. "La Parole Soufflée" and "The Theater of Cruelty and the Closure of Representation." In Derrida, *Writing and Difference,* trans. Alan Bass. Reprint. London: Routledge and Kegan Paul, 1985.

———. *The Truth in Painting,* trans. Geoff Bennington and Ian McLeod. Chicago: University of Chicago Press, 1987.

Dionysius, St., the Areopagite. *The Celestial and Ecclesiastical Hierarchy,* trans. Rev. John Parker. London: Skeffington and Son, 1894.

Eliade, Mircea. *The Forge and the Crucible,* trans. Stephen Corrin. 2nd ed.; Chicago: University of Chicago Press, 1978.

———. *Myth and Reality,* trans. Willard R. Trask. Reprint. New York: Harper and Row, 1975.

———. *Shamanism: Archaic Techniques of Ecstasy,* trans. Willard R. Trask. Princeton, N.J.: Princeton University Press, 1972.

Fernandez, James W. *Bwiti: An Ethnography of the Religious Imagination in Africa.* Princeton, N.J.: Princeton University Press, 1982.

———. *Persuasions and Performances: The Play of Tropes in Culture.* Bloomington: Indiana University Press, 1986.

Foster, Hal, ed. *The Anti-Aesthetic: Essays in Postmodern Culture.* Port Townsend, Wash.: Bay Press, 1983.

Foucault, Michel. *The Order of Things: An Archaeology of the Human Sciences*. London: Tavistock Publications, 1974.

Fried, Michael. "Three American Painters." In Francis Frascina and Charles Harrison, eds., *Modern Art and Modernism: A Critical Anthology*. London: Harper and Row, 1982. Reprinted from Fried, "Introduction," *Three American Painters: Kenneth Noland, Jules Olitski and Frank Stella*. Cambridge, Mass.: Fogg Art Museum, 1965.

Gablik, Suzi. *Has Modernism Failed?*. New York: Thames and Hudson, 1984.

———. *Progress in Art*. New York: Rizzoli International Publications, 1977.

Gadamer, Hans Georg. *Truth and Method*, trans. and ed. Garret Barden and John Cumming. New York: Seabury Press, 1975.

Gilmour, John C. "Anselm Kiefer: Postmodern Art and the Question of Technology." In Gary Shapiro, ed., *After the Future: Postmodern Times and Places*. Albany, N.Y.: SUNY Press, 1990.

———. "Original Representation and Anselm Kiefer's Postmodernism." *Journal of Aesthetics and Art Criticism* 46, no. 3 (spring, 1988): 341–350.

———. *Picturing the World*. Albany, N.Y.: SUNY Press, 1986.

Gimbutas, Marija. *The Goddesses and Gods of Old Europe: 6500–3500 B.C.* Berkeley: University of California Press, 1982.

Greenberg, Clement. "Modernist Painting." In Francis Frascina and Charles Harrison, eds., *Modern Art and Modernism: A Critical Anthology*. New York: Harper and Row, 1982. Reprinted from *Art and Literature* 4 (spring, 1965): 193–201.

Habermas, Jürgen. "Modernity—an Incomplete Project." In Hal Foster, ed., *The Anti-Aesthetic: Essays in Postmodern Culture*. Port Townsend, Wash.: Bay Press, 1983.

Hegel, G. W. F. *Reason in History: A General Introduction to the Philosophy of History*, trans. Robert S. Hartman. Indianapolis, Ind.: Bobbs-Merrill, 1953.

Heidegger, Martin. "The Age of the World Picture" and "The Question Concerning Technology." In Heidegger, *The Question Concerning Technology and Other Essays*, trans. William Lovitt. New York: Harper and Row, 1977.

———. "Building Dwelling Thinking" and "What Are Poets For?" In Heidegger, *Poetry, Language, Thought*, trans. and ed. Albert Hofstadter. New York: Harper and Row, 1971.

———. *The Will to Power as Art*. Vol. 1 of *Nietzsche*, trans. David Farrell Krell. San Francisco: Harper and Row, 1979.

Hinz, Berthold. *Art in the Third Reich*, trans. Robert Kimber and Rita Kimber. Oxford, Eng.: Basil Blackwell, 1979.

Inboden, Gudrun. "Exodus from Historical Time." In Paul Maenz and Gerd de Vries, eds., *Anselm Kiefer*. Köln: Galerie Paul Maenz, 1986.

Jameson, Fredric. "Postmodernism and Consumer Society." In Hal Foster, ed., *The Anti-Aesthetic: Essays on Postmodern Culture*. Port Townsend, Wash.: Bay Press, 1983.

————. "Postmodernism, or the Cultural Logic of Late Capitalism." *New Left Review* 146 (1984): 53–92.

Kandinsky, Vassily. *Concerning the Spiritual in Art*, trans. M. T. H. Sadler. New York: Dover, 1977.

Klossowski, Pierre. "Nietzsche's Experience of the Eternal Return." In David B. Allison, ed., *The New Nietzsche: New Styles of Interpretation*. New York: Dell Publishing Co., 1977.

Knapp, Bettina L. *Theater and Alchemy*. Detroit: Wayne State University Press, 1980.

Krauss, Rosalind. *The Originality of the Avant-Garde and Other Modernist Myths*. Cambridge, Mass.: MIT Press, 1985.

Kuspit, Donald. "Flak from the 'Radicals': The American Case Against Current German Painting." In Jack Cowart, ed., *Expressions: New Art from Germany*. St. Louis: St. Louis Art Museum, 1983.

"Lay of Volund [Wayland], The" In *The Poetic Edda*, trans. L. M. Hollander. 2nd ed.; Austin: University of Texas, 1962.

Lippard, Lucy R. *Overlay: Contemporary Art and the Art of Prehistory*. New York: Pantheon Books, 1983.

Lyotard, Jean-François. *The Postmodern Condition: A Report on Knowledge*, trans. Geoff Bennington and Brian Massumi. Manchester, Eng.: Manchester University Press, 1984.

Madoff, Steven Henry. "Anselm Kiefer: A Call to Memory." *Art News* 86, no. 8 (1987): 125–130.

Maenz, Paul, and Gerd de Vries, eds. *Anselm Kiefer*. Köln: Galerie Paul Maenz, 1986.

Margolis, Joseph. *Culture and Cultural Entities: Toward a New Unity of Science*. Boston: D. Reidel, 1984.

————. "Postscript on Modernism and Postmodernism, Both." *Theory, Culture and Society* 6, no. 1 (February, 1989): 5–30.

————. "Reinterpreting Interpretation." *Journal of Aesthetics and Art Criticism* 47, no. 3 (summer, 1989): 237–251.

Mauss, Marcel. *The Gift: Forms and Functions of Exchange in Archaic Societies*, trans. Ian Cunnison. Glencoe, Ill.: Free Press, 1954.

Nietzsche, Friedrich. *Beyond Good and Evil*, trans. R. J. Hollingdale. Reprint. New York: Penguin Books, 1981.

———. *The Birth of Tragedy*, trans. Walter Kaufmann. New York: Random House, 1967.

———. *The Case of Wagner*, trans. Walter Kaufmann. New York: Vintage, 1967.

———. *The Gay Science*, trans. Walter Kaufmann. New York: Random House, 1974.

———. *On the Genealogy of Morals*, trans. Walter Kaufmann and R. J. Hollingdale. New York: Random House, 1967.

———. *Thus Spoke Zarathustra*, trans. R. J. Hollingdale. Reprint. New York: Penguin Books, 1969.

———. *Twilight of the Idols*, trans. R. J. Hollingdale. Reprint. New York: Penguin Books, 1977.

———. *The Will to Power*, ed. Walter Kaufmann, trans. Walter Kaufmann and R. J. Hollingdale. Reprint. New York: Random House, 1968.

Phillipson, Michael. *Painting, Language, and Modernity*. London: Routledge and Kegan Paul, 1985.

Rorty, Richard. *Contingency, Irony, and Solidarity*. Cambridge, Eng.: Cambridge University Press, 1989.

Rosenthal, Mark, ed. *Anselm Kiefer*. Chicago: Art Institute; Philadelphia: Philadelphia Museum of Art, 1987.

Seymour, Anne. "Notes on the Plates." *Anselm Kiefer Watercolours, 1970–1982*. London: Anthony d'Offay Gallery, 1983.

Steinberg, Leo. *Other Criteria: Confrontations with Twentieth Century Art*. New York: Oxford University Press, 1972.

Stephanson, Anders. "Interview with Fredric Jameson." *Flash Art* 131 (December, 1986/January, 1987): 69–73.

Vernant, Jean-Pierre. *Myth and Thought Among the Ancient Greeks*. Boston: Routledge and Kegan Paul, 1983.

Vernant, Jean-Pierre, and Pierre Vidal-Naquet. *Tragedy and Myth in Ancient Greece*, trans. Janet Lloyd. Atlantic Highlands, N.J.: Humanities Press, 1981.

Index